Other available titles from Dr. Nathaniel Stampley, Sr.

Parables of The Kingdom

Introduction to Homiletics

Understanding Spiritual Gifts and Calling to Ministry

Bible Commentary

On

Wisdom Literature

**(Job, Psalms, Proverbs, Ecclesiastes,
and Song of Solomon)**

Copyright © 2017 Nathaniel Stampley

Spiritscribe Publishing, LLC
P.O. Box 2241
Humble, Texas 77347
www.spiritscribepublishing.com
(832) 445-6229

Stampley Ministries, Inc.
1036 W. Atkinson Avenue
Milwaukee, Wisconsin 53206
Phone: (414) 949-7568
Website: stampleyministries.org
Email: stampleyministries@gmail.com

ISBN 978-0-692-86077-9

Bible Commentary On Wisdom Literature

(Job, Psalms, Proverbs, Ecclesiastes, and Song of Solomon)

Dr. Nathaniel J. Stampley, Sr.

Acknowledgments

I am a student of history, and this includes humbly submitting the original man and woman came from the place we call Africa, *The Motherland.* I carry the DNA of this distinguished ancestry. Nonetheless, this journey has allowed me to discover my true essence is lodged beneath the physical body in a sacred place called the Soul/Spirit. Putting it another way, race is not scientific and was never highlighted in antiquity, but the truth has to be housed and implanted within the human arena.

Initially, I planned to present the entire Bible Commentary (Old and New Testament). However, after several years of writing, I am pleased to limit these commentaries to the Old Testament simply because she represents the foundation for understanding the New Testament.

This book will provide inspirational and informational materials regarding the Wisdom Literature Section of the Protestant Bible. Subsequently, we will share commentaries on the Law, History, and Prophets. Eventually, we will compile them all together, thus giving a refreshed revelatory perspective of the people, places and situations expressed in Old Testament Literature.

I was truly blessed with parents who were spiritually, ethically and practically grounded. They lived an exemplary life before my siblings and the community where we resided, Baton Rouge, Louisiana and for this I am eternally grateful.

Dr. Arenia C. Mallory, my mentor was a distinguished educator, humanitarian, and international traveler. I was blessed to sit under her tutelage at Saints Academy and Junior College, Lexington, Mississippi during the years of 1967-71. The school's motto was, "Walk in dignity, talk in dignity, and live in dignity." I am eternally grateful for what she poured in me.

I love discovering and presenting information in a scholarly and inspirational manner. This compilation is the result of many years of intense studying, observations, international traveling and what we call *Mother Wit*. I love quoting and extracting from others who have come before and those who are yet with us, because at the end of the day,I want to see more people informed and accountable. I am always inspired by this quote, "Knowledge makes a man unfit to be a slave," Fredrick Douglas.

I want to thank my printer, Spiritscribe Publishing for the professional and courteous service he has rendered. I want to thank Heritage International Ministries Church of God in Christ and Least of These International Ministries, where I serve as their spiritual leader for supporting and listening to these lessons over the years. I want to thank my family for listening, encouraging and embracing a life of faith alongside me.

Lastly, I want to give special thanks to my lovely wife (married since 1972) for the critical eyes and finishing touch she brings to each of my publications. She is a spiritual gem and represents grace, beauty and wisdom in the truest sense. I appreciate the ancient texts, but I understand their true meaning every time I see the Queen Motherly spirit displayed in her.

Introduction to Wisdom Literature (Ketuvim)

Poetry is a unique form of artistic and creative expressions that gives us a sense of the mindset and experiences of an ethnic group during good and bad times. Putting it another way, wisdom expressed through poetry reflects the accumulative-cultural experience or ethos of a people. These cultural values validate and distinguish an individual with a group.

Altogether there are five books placed in this category: **Job, Psalms, Proverbs, Ecclesiastes,** and **Song of Solomon.** Each is written in a unique, poetic style conveying truth and is also commonly called wisdom literature.

The first book (Job) presents an interesting account of a righteous man who was falsely accused and destined to face prolonged suffering. Therefore, he lost everything i.e. family, wealth, health, and respect in the community. He sought answers by asking pertinent questions to God. Finally, God speaks and reminds him who is in control and restores all he had and more.

Psalms is the longest and most widely read book in the Bible. This composite of hymnals teach us how to worship and praise God in spite the challenges we face. The Psalms reminds me of the American Negro Spirituals simply because of the creative manner African Americans crafted creative and inspirational lyrics during the inhumane period known as American Chattel Slavery. There are lamenting, exuberant, thanksgiving, pilgrimage, enthronement and wisdom psalms, etc. covering a wide range of human experiences. Psalms 100 gives us a comprehensive view of what God expects from us. Psalms is a display of a vibrant faith.

The book of Proverbs gives us a wide range of maxims and wise sayings. The contrast is drawn between opting to be wise or foolish. Adhering to a life of righteousness will be complimented with wisdom and favor. It should also be noted this book contains many of the ancient proverbs already established along the Nile Valley Civilizations.

The book of Ecclesiastes stands out for me due to her philosophical (asking questions) rather than theological (providing answers) format. Otherwise, perhaps we may label this book theosophy. Nonetheless, the fundamental question centers around man and woman discovering the essence of life while discovering life is compared to a vapor or vanity (fleeting moment). Wisdom is the principle objective, but you will also discover both the righteous and unrighteous will suffer and face death; therefore, we must position ourselves to get a firm grip of who we are and what is most important in life.

The last book (Song of Solomon) presents a series of intimate poems describing the simplistic and complex relationship between a man and woman. Ultimately, we should recognize love is a spiritual and eternal entity, whereby all of us have the capacity to embrace and express love. Even more importantly, each of us should love God with all our hearts and souls.

Collectively, the Wisdom/Poetic Literature gives us a wholesome and diverse perspective of human experiences both within the covenant community, Israel, and beyond. Wisdom emanates from God and represents a proven path. The outline for each book is taken from the English Standard Version Bible, and (unless otherwise noted) the scriptures I use will be presented in the same translation.

Lastly, you will observe various shifts in the format for each book. This shift is a good thing because it demonstrates spiritual growth, continual learning, and specific revelations regarding the text. I cannot emphasize enough how important it is for you as readers to remain open to new information that will foster appreciation for the sacred text.

Outline Book of Job

I. Prologue: Job's Character and the Circumstances of His Test (1:1-2:13)

A. The Integrity of Job (1:1-5)

B. The first test (1:6-22)

1. The challenge in heaven (1:6-12)

2. The loss of family and possessions (1:13-19)

3. Job's confession and confidence (1:20-22)

C. The second test (2:1-10)

1. The challenge in heaven (2:1-6)

2. Job's affliction and confession (2:7-10)

D. Job's comforters (2:11-13)

II. Dialogue: Job, His Suffering, and His Standing before God (3:1-42:6)

A. Job: despair for the day of his birth (3:1-26)

1. Introduction (3:1-2)

2. Job curses his birth (3:3-10)

3. Job longs for rest (3:11-19)

4. Job laments his suffering (3:20-26)

B. The friends and Job: can Job be right before God? (4:1-25:6)

   1. First cycle (4:1-14:22)

      a. Eliphaz: Can mortal man be in the right before God (4:1-25:6)

      b. Job: Life is futile (6:1-7:21)

      c. Bildad: the wisdom of the sages (8:1-22)

      d. Job: How can a mortal be just before God? (9:1-10:22)

      e. Zophar: repent (11:1-20)

      f. Job: a challenge to the "wisdom" of his friends (12:1-14:22)

   2. Second cycle (15:1-21:34)

      a. Eliphaz: Job's words condemn him (15:1-35)

      b. Job: hope for a sufferer (16:1-17:16)

      c. Bildad: punishment for the wicked (18:1-21)

      d. Job: my Redeemer lives (19:1-29)

      e. Zophar: the wicked will die (20:1-29)

      f. Job: the wicked prosper (21:1-34)

   3. Third cycle (22:1-25:6)

      a. Eliphaz: Job is guilty (22:1-30)

3. The second challenge: understanding justice and power (40:6-41:34)

4. Job's response: submission (42:1-6)

III. Epilogue: The vindication, Intercession, and Restoration of Job (42:7-17)

A. The Lord rebukes the three friends (42:7-9)

B. The Lord restores Job (42:10-17)

Introduction to Job

This book is simply amazing and timeless. The author is anonymous, yet the writer is abreast of Hebrew culture and customs. The book encompasses broad and diverse categories or subjects. For example, the status of man, universe, seasons, and wisdom are all discussed.

The story of Job applies to man and woman throughout the global community. Life will always present good and evil, righteous and unrighteous, and faithful and unfaithful. Job should not be idolized or romanticized as if he always said and did the right thing. Contrarily, Job displayed loyalty to God, but he said inappropriate words displaying questionable character during his weakest moment. However, he fulfilled a purpose. We will also learn the power and ultimate benefits of forgiveness. This book truly illustrates you do not know as much as you think you know about spiritual and natural affairs. You can literally have a pleasant life before it is suddenly interrupted, what do you do, then?

I. Prologue: Job's Character and the Circumstances of His Test (1:1-2:13)

Chapter 1: The opening chapters compliment Job's character and introduce a series of tests. Righteousness is a virtue or vindication extended from God to the man and woman who submit to spiritual authority. From the off-set it is established, Job is blessed.

Meanwhile, there emerges another storyline unfolding as it relates to God and Satan. One day, Satan (a fallen angel and adversary) appeared before the Almighty while the other heavenly beings and Sons of God also appeared in the midst. If he was not there to worship, then what was his purpose for being in this holy place?

Apparently, Satan maintained access to God just like a wayward child is usually allowed to enter the parent's home. Satan is recognized and questioned, but he is readily identified by his demeanor or characteristic of *going to and from on the earth, and from walking up and down it.* The conversation seemed general, but then it shifts to something specific, namely God offering or suggesting the testing of Job. Therefore, Satan is given permission to test Job through these attacks upon his life, indirectly.

For example, in a short span (1:13-19) the following four things occurred:

- ➢ Sabeans killed Job's servants.
- ➢ Fire from heaven consumed sheep and servants.
- ➢ Chaldeans raided camel and servants.

➢ All of Job's children (10) were killed during a great wind storm.

In each of these cases, a witness lived to tell the story. Despite these painful realities, Job simply said, "The Lord gave, and the Lord has taken away; blessed be the name of the Lord."

From time to time, it is good to discuss history and geography. For example, the Sabeans are identified in scripture and history as descendants of Kush/ Ethiopia. They are identified with ancient kingdoms of Seba and Son of Raamah (Genesis 10:7; 1 Chronicles 1:9 & Ezekiel 27:22; 38:13). In addition, they are referred to as descendants of Abraham via marriage with Keturah (Genesis 25:3). Even further, there appears to be clans of Sabeans both in Kush and Arabia. As you can see, this sort of information is seldom or deliberately neglected in most commentaries.

On the other hand, the Chaldeans are historically identified with Southern Babylon. Most noted Abraham comes from Ur of Chaldea (Genesis Chapter 11 & 12). Sumer and Mesopotamia are associated with Chaldea. In both instances, the Sabeans and Chaldeans we are referring to are ancient African-Asiatic ancestry thus causing the reader to claim Job is more than likely Black with African ancestry.

Chapter 2: The chapter unfolds by introducing and implying a reoccurring pattern taking place, whereby the Sons of God, along with Satan, appear before the Lord in the form of a heavenly council. Once again, Satan describes his mission and God mentioned Job; however, this is done after all the unpleasant experiences in chapter one. Nevertheless, in this dialogue, Satan makes sure he has permission to physically attack Job because Satan was confident Job would denounce and curse God by so doing.

Shortly thereafter, Job's health had fallen, and he looked horrible with sores all over his body. His appearance was so detestable until his wife suggested cursing God and die. Of course, he rebuked her, and she becomes a silent factor throughout the story.

Chapter two concludes (verses 11-13) by introducing several friends: Eliphaz (Temanite), Bildad (Shuhite) and Zophar (Naamathite). They visited Job, sitting seven full days without saying a word. The ethnicity of these men is interesting and is traced back to Abraham and his descendants. It should be noted the friends initially came to comfort and not condemn: however, it suddenly changed upon hearing Job talk about things. Plus, the friends sparked an interesting and prolonged dialogue based upon accusations.

II: Dialogue: Job's Suffering, and Standing before God (3:1-42:6)

This section is somewhat prolonged because there are several dialogue, cycles, and challenges with suffering involving Job, his friends, and God. The writer does not depict Job cursing God, nor does he curse his deplorable condition. Generally speaking, a curse is an expression or pronouncement of misfortune. Verses 3-10 describe discomfort and disdain about his life and life in general for those who suffer. However in verses 11-19, he is sighing and longing to find rest, including, once again, questioning why he was born (verse 16). The lamenting continues with him even longing for death, but it does not occur. An interesting quote that has sparked continual discussion is noted when he said, "For the thing that I fear comes upon me and what I dread befalls me." What was it he feared and dreaded most? Perhaps, he was concerned about losing God's favor, property, family, and this will just begin to help us understand his plight.

Friends of Job Challenge His Integrity before God (4:1-25:6)

The text gives us no clue regarding when or how this friendship started. Three friends are introduced representing several, ethnic backgrounds, and diverse personalities. Remember, it is part of the character and nature of Satan to bring accusation. Therefore, the first friend (Eliphaz) begins his discourse in the framework of portraying a scenario of Job's guilt because the innocent should not suffer. Perhaps, this chapter can be summarized in verse 17, which says, "Can mortal man be in the right with God? Can a man be pure before God?"

Chapter 5 Eliphaz continues his discourse permeating around the same theme, namely, can a man do right before God? Verses 3-4 refers to Job's suffering and family due to the disfavor of God. The accusations are pointed and categorized. For example, he admonished Job to seek God because He is the Creator. The lecture or rebuke continues in verse 17 by alluding that God's chastisement has a purpose for those who seek counsel.

Job Responds by saying Life is Futile (6:1-7:21)

For the most part, none of us will tolerate lectures in accusations without a response. Job's initial reply justified his complaint as just, but here is a man wrestling and seeking answers. Note, in verses 9 & 10, he opted for death, yet states he is faithful to God. Also, verse 10 is a response to Eliphaz's comment (5:17f) alluding to unfaithfulness to God. Job continues his response by alluding to forgiveness, reproof, and justice before God.

Chapter 7 continues Job's discourse by depicting a hopeless man. He draws from nature & culture, such as a slave, worms, and dirt. The night seemed prolonged and Sheol, place of deceased bodies, is mentioned. He wanted to be silent, but the agony prompted him to keep talking (vs. 11). There is reference to the sea and the monster.

The frustration and searching is mounting, and take note in verses 17-21. Life for Job is a breath. He wants to know what man is. Job then suggested sin is the cause of this suffering and plead for mercy. It is simply amazing to see all this unfold, yet Job was never informed. Instead, God knew what was spiritually invested and, in the end, would yield a great return.

Bildad Speaks: Job Should Repent (8:1-22)

The dialogue is underway between Job and his friends. In this chapter, Bildad (the second friend) is building up an argument, pointing the finger strongly, and encouraging Job to repent. He suggested asking for justice from God, and apparently alluded as fact that his children had transgressed and died as a result of it. He goes on to draw analogies of distinguished fathers and papyrus plants flourishing in an environment God had created. Therefore, if you are blameless (vs. 20) as the opening text mentioned, then conditions should not be as they are.

Job Replies (9:1-10:22)

Job is miserable and like a typical man felt obligated to respond to this accusation. Initially, he tends to agree with the notion of our inability to stand before a holy God, but more so, who can defend his or her self before the Almighty? He goes on to describe the sovereignty of God, not only in regards to righteousness but also in scenes of nature like the constellations (Bear, Orion, & Pleiades). He is wrestling with an awesome God and a life he thought was blameless. Nonetheless, Job's lack of spiritual clarity also claims God has ordered this upon his life (vs. 17). This predicament caused Job to view life is swift, and condemnation is yet his reality, even if he claimed innocence. He is longing for relief and an explanation, but there appears to be no arbiter (vs. 33) to assist him before God.

Job's plea continues in chapter 10, but it seems to have shifted from responding to his accuser to that of speaking directly to God. This section is passionate and gives us a sense of how much pain he was facing. Job utilized a series of anthropomorphic or human characteristics before God. Verse 7 gives us a sense of his dilemma, but the dialogue goes on. He acknowledged life comes from God but questioned rather or not it would have been better to die at birth than to be disgraced like this. As you can see, Job is not the romanticized character displayed in religious circles, yet we learn from his reality. Instead, life has taken a toll, and he is speaking out of anguish and trying to understand this relationship he had with God.

Zophar Speaks: You Deserve Worse (11:1-20)

Now, we have the third friend speak within the first cycle. This accusation takes on another approach by suggesting Job is putting forth empty words and everyone should be able to see his suffering is a punishment. Verses 4-6 put it plainly, Job is deemed guilty. Zophar goes on to reaffirm the wisdom of God while alluding to Job's worthlessness (vs. 11). The remaining verses (11-20) admonished Job to open his heart and raise his hand before God, thereby, a change will occur in your life.

Job Responded by Challenging the Wisdom of his friends (12:1-14:22)

For the third time, Job deemed it necessary to respond to these accusations. In this instance, he reminds Zophar he is not inferior, and they are not the only ones with understanding. Once upon a time, it seemed obvious Job was blameless and God answered his prayer, but now the tables have turned, and he is displayed a laughingstock. A series of questions are asked once again by drawing from nature, wherein he concludes the hand of God has done this to him.

The remaining verses (13-25) give an impressive discourse regarding the wisdom of God. Powerful nations and men are often stripped of power whether religious or civic, and they are pleading for the mercies of God, such as Job's reality. Therefore, the friend's assessments are ill-advised or inadequate, but there is no doubt God is orchestrating these experiences.

Chapter 13 continues Job's response but make no mistake, his hope rests in God. Once again, Job shifts from speaking directly to his friends but rather make his petitions to God. He is irritated with these friends and it shows (vs. 4-5) and they are called liars. The mastery of words being fused together as if Job is in a court is clearly noted. For example, the courts are designed to hear presentations on both sides and then make a ruling. Verse 12 reminds the friends their practical illustrations are useless. Verse 15 is a Biblical Classic and brings us back to focus on Job's integrity and the reason why God allowed this to happen.

The case before God and his friends continues, and interestingly Job makes two requests from God (vs. 20-21), but the request is not met at this juncture.

Chapter 14 has surfaced in the Church as one of the favorite scriptures during funerals. Job continues his response to the third friend. Death is a painful and persistent reality while delivery from a mother's womb until that day is brief. He goes on to illustrate the track through life can be challenging and perplexed.

Job draws upon the life of a tree and man. This analogy is often used in both Old and New Testaments. The life of man and the tree is drawn upon simply because they both have roots, and they are connected to life-giving sources. Sheol (the grave) is mentioned again as the depository of the corpse. However, in this instance, a theological discussion regarding resurrection emerged in lieu of the question: "If a man dies, shall he live again?" Job longs to be renewed in this life, but the agony of life is prolonged.

The mountains, rocks, and water are utilized in a majestic and teachable manner, but it seems as though the hope of man is destroyed. Job cannot get a grip as to why God allows these painful realities, including dying in misery, to occur.

It would seem to us enough has been said from his friends and Job, but this is not the case. The discourse goes on with accusations and responses along with insightful comments on both parts. Nevertheless, we will also observe insightful comments in the midst of these exchanges.

2. Second Cycle (15:1-21:34) & Eliphaz Accuses: Job Does Not Fear God

Chapter 15 opens with the first friend (Eliphaz) beginning the second cycle of accusations against Job by declaring he does not fear God. This posture clearly suggests he is wise and qualified to make this claim.

Verses 1-5 describe Job's words as windy and void of substance. Verse 4 states this claim, emphatically. He goes on to say his mouth is associated with an unrighteous man who automatically condemns himself.

The crafty speech grounded in debasing words continues in verses 7-16. Take note of the series of questions as if Job is a novice in the faith. This inappropriate questioning and accusation further supports his thoughts of Job: abominable, and corrupt. It is obvious he is spiritually unaligned, especially when we take note of his perspective in verse 15.

Verses 17-35 give us a prolonged discourse regarding what he claims to know through experience. Verse 20 supports his premise by reminding him the wicked (not the righteous) suffers. He follows with precise details regarding the path of the unrighteous. Rebellion against God results in consequences such as in battle, desolate cities, poverty, and even death. Verse 32 clearly tells Job the life of the unrighteous will be miserable before he dies.

Job Replies: Miserable Comforters Are You (Chapters 16-17)

It takes a whole lot of discipline to remain silent after strong and piercing accusation. Therefore, Job responds in chapter 16 by declaring all three of them are miserable comforters (verse 2). He goes on to say he could say the same about them if matters were opposite you, but that does not make it right.

Job shifts in verse 8 and the following by reminding them it is obvious the Most High has orchestrated this misery. However, Job's perspectives at certain interval may be discussed theologically speaking. For example, verse 9 indicates the suffering is the result of God's hate. He goes on speaking of his anguish and fate throughout verse 17.

However, 18-22 Job shifts from all the anguish and suffering. Verse 19 is an interesting viewpoint in that he reaffirms God is his faithful witness although He seems to be silent at the moment. He ends by reiterating what his friends are doing and the certainty of death at hand.

Chapter 17 continues Job's response to his friend Eliphaz. In verses 1-4 it appears Job is searching for answers by addressing God. His spirit is broken, and the friends are displayed as mockers.

Job describes himself as the example of pity and disgrace in the community he was once esteemed in Verses 6-16. He is keenly aware God is his source, yet he is troubled by his reality, suffering, and the way he is perceived.

Bildad Speaks: God Punishes the Wicked (Chapter 18)

If you and I were involved, perhaps we would have ended this a long time ago. Instead, Bildad initiates another round of accusation. It is simply amazing how far people can and will go when it come from a self-righteous perspective. To him, Job is wicked and assumes they are stupid (verse 3). The wicked is not only punished but will be entrapped by his deceit. He gives analogies that are clever and suggests punishment such as traps, terror, and rope awaits him. The wicked will be abruptly taken from his dwelling, and memory of him will vanish.

Job Replies: My Redeemer Lives (Chapter 19)

Job seems to keep tab of these attacks and accusations (10 times). He asks why do they ridicule him but then find resolve in saying even if I erred it was not against anyone (verse 4). Verses 5-12 seem to indicate God has ganged up on him, and there is no escape.

He goes on to indicate (verse 13) his brothers i.e. family and friends are all alien to his suffering. It got so bad that even the children disrespected him, leaving him feeling all alone. However, he seems to always return to the center of his being as reflected in verse 25, a biblical classic, "For I know that my Redeemer lives, and at the last he will stand upon the earth." Despite his prolonged suffering, he always found a way to put things in perspective.

Zophar Speaks: The Wicked Will Suffer (Chapter 20)

This nonsense or saga continues with the third friend speaking in the 2nd cycle. He too assumes the same posture: Job is wicked. However, he appears to be anxious (verse 2) to talk. He goes on giving illustrations by drawing upon wisdom and the wicked. In essence, the wicked days are numbered, and his memory will be short-lived.

Verses 10-21 states the wicked and their offspring will not be able to enjoy what they have acquired. He emphasized this point by describing his body, food, and the cobra that will poison him.

The remaining verses convey the wicked is under divine scrutiny. The food will not benefit him, and his body will be laden with sickness. The heavens and earth will testify against the wicked, and there will be no mistake: God is punishing the wicked man.

Job Replies: The Wicked Do Prosper (Chapter 21)

Job's reply concludes the 2nd cycle of dialog. Verses 1-6 show Job plead for his friend to listen at him despite his fail and unattractive state.

Verses 7-16 presents a discourse suggesting the wicked prosper, including living without the judgment or interruption he is experiencing. He goes on to say, as it appears to him, the wicked disrespect God and yet lives (1-14)

Verses 17-21 reveal Job is challenging the remarks Bildad made earlier (18:5-6) by desiring to know how often this is manifested.

Job realizes God is infinite but wrestles with the various forms of death (verses 23-16). The remaining verses (27-34) share more of Job's response to his friend and concerns for the fate and destiny of the wicked one, including after he dies. He concludes this chapter by reminding them their words are empty and they represent falsehood.

Third Cycle: (Chapter 22:1-25:6

Eliphaz Speaks Regarding Job's Wickedness is Great
(Chapter 22:1-30)

In this segment, we are about to see a systematic and persistent attempt to prove once and for all Job has displayed a pattern of wickedness. Verses 2-4 open with several questions and commentaries. In essence, he concludes Job is deceiving him by claiming to be wise.

Verses 5-11 accentuate the charges in a more precise manner against Job. He is accused of taking advantage of his brothers, not caring for the disinherited, and neglecting the widows and fatherless. Therefore, Job is getting what he deserved as a wicked man.

The remaining verses give us some interesting theological views. For example, we note the farness and nearness of God. The path of the righteous and unrighteous is described; however, the righteous seem to always be rewarded. Verse 21 admonished Job to confess or agree with God in order to be forgiven. It is presumed Job's pride has caused his dilemma and a lowly state of repentance will usher a change.

Job Replies: Where is God (Chapters 23 & 24)

The cycle or, shall we say, the drama continues by asking a profound and philosophical question. Perhaps, the question is channeled at his friends more so than God. Here again, we come across a Biblical Classic. Bitterness and failure to explain will cause you search for answers.

It appears in Job's premise God is not with him, and he longs to be in His presence. It is further suggested the upright man has access to God. He goes on to describe the four positions: forward, backward, left, and right. However, he does not recognize God's presence.

Despite this emptiness, Job presents his case before the Almighty and suggests just as gold is tried and purified, so will he do the same. The remaining verses 13-17 Job realized God's faithfulness and his dependence upon Him.

Chapter 24 opens with a couple of questions such as we commonly experience in a court room. Essentially, he seeks to understand the role of judgment (commonly called the *Day of the Lord)* because it appears the wicked is getting by with his or her evil.

Verses 2-12 put forth a series of unethical behaviors carried out by the wicked, such as moving the landmarks; stealing livestock; exploiting the elderly; mistreating the poor; taking over the vineyard; enslavement and moaning of the oppressed.

Verses 13-17 disclose the transgressors by using the metaphor light as consciousness. For example, the murderer and thief carry out his evil ways in the dark. The adulterer or unfaithful one moves about prior to daylight. Simply stated, God is not asleep.

Verses 18-20 present a challenge regarding Job's intent simply because it appears he is putting forth phrases that compliments his friend perspectives, initially. Nonetheless, water and lack of same are associated with something swiftly occurring and causing a drought. Subsequently, death occurs and leaves a trail of sorrow similar to a broken tree.

The wicked behavior seems endless. Furthermore, they have no regards for the barren woman and widow. Nevertheless, it appears God does nothing to them. Evil seems prevalent, yet the same seem to have security and exaltation. He ends the chapter by challenging his friends to disprove his assessment.

Bildad Speaks: Man cannot be Righteous (Chapter 25)

Bildad speaks in the same order he has done, previously. The chapter is relatively short but consistent with accusation. He starts off by reminding Job righteousness and sovereignty comes from God. Therefore, man (a finite being) lacks the ability to be righteous. He makes reference to the stars and moon not being the brightest in the heaven despite both of their majesties. He concludes man is like a maggot and *Son of Man* a worm.

Job Replies: God's Majesty is Unsearchable (Chapter 26)

Despite Job's unfavorable position, he remains grounded or aware. He seemed to accuse his friend of not doing the very things they accused him of not doing: namely, assisting the poor or disinherited. The remaining verses (5-15) give us further insights into the theological views of Job. For example, Sheol (death) and Abaddon (abodes of the deceased) are subjected to the Almighty. The directions and elements in nature are subject to God. The zodiac and astrological spheres are under the watchful eyes of God. The whispers and loud noises are subject to his command. Therefore, these remarks reflect a man who truly knows God although he cannot thoroughly explain his current fate.

Job Continues: I Will Maintain My Integrity (Chapter 27)

Job is simply amazing as he respond to his friends while wrestling with explaining what God is doing. This spiritual encounter is played out in a legal display of words and concepts.

There are times in life circumstances i.e. courts or family matters that may cause you to seek for an explanation. Despite his inability to fully explain verses 2-4 emphatically states there is an acknowledgment of God as well as he refuse to be deceitful.

Verses 5-6 he alludes to there may be some truth in the friend accusations. However, he confirms what was initially said about him (2:3), holding fast his integrity. In other words enough has been said and done that would have caused the average person to *throw in the towel*, figuratively speaking.

Verses 7-23 put forth an interesting theological discussion and textual criticism. For some, it appears as if the verbiage reflects the tone and beliefs of his friends accusing Job. For example, you might observe the following: Plight of the ungodly; the manner by which the Almighty operates; the wicked and his off-springs; Judgment regarding the wicked depicted in terror and the wind of life etc.

Job Continues: Where is Wisdom? (Chapter 28)

At the end of this chapter I will share a sermon entitled, *Wisdom and the Secret Places.* The overall focus of this chapter displays Job searching for answers regarding wisdom. However, he is convinced wisdom outweighs anything else in life and she is the sole property of God.

The chapter can be studied by viewing it in three parts, namely, verses 1-11 deals with the valuable treasures in the earth and verses 12-22 deals with wisdom and understanding is far more valuable than all the jewelry put together and lastly verses 23-28 share Job's awareness that only God fully knows wisdom and understanding and fearing or worshipping Him exclusively give you access to these benefits.

As you can see Job makes a radical shift from the perspectives shared in the previous verse. Reference to Ethiopia (Kush) is another reminder of an esteemed place from antiquity that is in the Motherland, Africa.

Sermons: "Wisdom and The Secret Place"
(Job 28: 1 -8) 9/20/09; 8/26/12& 6/8/13)

Let me start this message with a story about a minister who happened to be passing through a field where he saw a very old man planting an oak tree. "Why are you planting that tree?" he asked.

"You surely don't expect to live long enough to see the acorn grow up to an oak tree?"

"No," replied the wise old man, "My ancestors planted trees, not for themselves, but for us in order that we might enjoy their shade and their fruit. I am doing likewise for those who will come after me."

Listen to these enlightening words and allow your heart and ears to receive this message. "Vision without action is merely a dream. Action without vision just passes the time. Vision with action can change the world." (Anonymous)

Negative and positive energies are all around us. There are definite and clear indicators pointing us in the right direction while there are distractions luring you down a deceptive path. Do you know the method or path to obtain the truth and realize what is best for you? Mistakes and unfortunate circumstances (so we call them) are merely stepping-stones and wake-up calls to embrace wisdom and the entrance to the door of spiritual secrecy.

33

Positioning and timing plays an important role in you truly becoming spiritually mature or spiritually crippled for life. I admit I have made mistakes without handling things the best, even after establishing a relationship with Christ. However, I refuse to remain stuck and allow grace (opportunity) and knowledge pass me by. We must learn from our mistakes and graciously move along or be dragged along in life.

In today's message, we are about to become acquainted with perhaps the most interesting character in the entire Bible. Job represents a classic example of what it means to study both mystery and truth. One day, he had everything i.e. status, family, priest, wealth, and he was blameless. Suddenly, he literally lost all he had and wanted to die. Painful experiences can and will push you to opt for death over life or discouragement over inspiration.

The book of Job permeates around a profound lesson regarding the manner in which the righteous can and will suffer. We do not know who wrote this book, and we are missing a precise date for compilation. However, some suggest it was pre-exilic and post-exilic. The scriptures introduce Job without mentioning any ancestral reference, and the story ends without any information about where or when he is buried. Actually, he is simply identified as a blameless (above reproach) and upright man.

Job is challenged physically and spiritually beyond what the average person would expect and possibly would be able to endure. Nonetheless, through all his adversities when it was all said and done, he became a better person who understood more about the mind of God as well as the behavior of people.

Now, it appears to me that a disproportionate number of people are living an unproductive and unfulfilled life stemming from allowing themselves complacence with being merely religious and living routine lives due to Satan having masterfully blocked and interrupted the path leading to wisdom and the sacred chamber of the Holy One.

Let us take a few moments and comment on our text because it contains treasures for life. In Chapters 26-31, we observe Job engage in a lengthy response to one of his friends (Bildad). The conversation seems to focus on God's unsearchable riches and wisdom disbursed throughout creation. More specifically, Chapter 28 puts forth a profound question: "Where is wisdom?" However and more profoundly, there are a couple of key question: But where wisdom shall be found? And where is the place of understanding?

In verses 1 and 2, the writer draws a poetic scenario of mining fields in order to attract our attention to the reality surrounding the hidden and revealing aspects of life. He starts by presenting precious minerals. You can only find gold, silver, iron, and copper beneath the earth, but the miner must labor by excavating, collecting, washing, and refining the product in order to tap these resources.

Verse 3 instructs and challenges us to overcome fear of the darkness (ignorance) and pursue wisdom just like you see ore (a combination of minerals extracted from metals. In other words, it requires skill and diligence to overcome the gloom and darkness associated with these minerals, but the finished product will cause you to rejoice.

Verse 4 discloses the writer refers to a shaft, which serve as a stream having starting and stopping points with intervals. Likewise, a shaft is referred to as a gully, wherein a vent is placed along a narrow path vertically and horizontally. Interestingly, the writer shares several metaphorical uses of the term i.e. away from where anyone lives, forgotten by travelers, and away from humankind. This place with abandoned appearance can serve as the connection for genuine worship places.

Verses 5-6 remind us the earth provides the food for nourishment: wheat, barley, maize, and beans, etc, yet the element of fire is deeper beneath the surface. In addition, the same earth happens to be the haven for precious stones/rocks that shelters the sapphires and gold dust.

Now, we come to our key verses, 7-8. All of you are traveling and will end up somewhere productive or unproductive. The writer skillfully paints a picture by shifting from the precious minerals to the animal kingdom and drives the thought home. Yes, there is a path or road for man and woman where even the keen eyes, power and grace of the falcon who is marveled in the sky as well as the courageous and domineering lion who is respected on earth cannot tread upon.

In other words, God has made provision for a hidden and sacred place whereby you can have the ultimate experience of worship. You see, there are many things in this life designed to frighten you and disrupt the rhythmic flow of living. This depiction or sacred place is commonly referred to as the *third dimension* or the *holy of holiest.*

As you can see, Job skillfully showed us all of the activities and preparation that went on in the outer areas of life. We engage ourselves in a variety of activities such as marriage, children, employment, community, government, safety, health and religion etc. We are living in an age that is moving at a fast pace without seriously stopping to see where are the benefits of all these comforts.

According to verses 7 and 8, western society has romanticized living with the beast and offers excuses for living with it. Let me define the term beast from a scriptural and theological perspective. The Old Testament Hebrew term, *Behemah* denotes domesticated and undomesticated animals. However, by the time, we get to the Old Testament Prophets and New Testament theology it exclusively refers to an untamed, wild, anti-Christ or adversarial reality causing problems for the righteous.

Look around the global community, and you will see a beastly spirit expressed in personal and collective violence:

> ➢ It is beastly to degrade women and abuse little children.

> ➢ It is beastly to glut and disregard healthy eating and exercising.

> It is beastly to deceive and exploit others for selfish gains.

> It is beastly to walk around arrogantly and cause terror and intimidation for those whom you meet.

> It is beastly to fight against righteousness and act as if you have done nothing wrong.

> It is beastly to spread venomous lies. As you can see a beastly spirit is will ultimately cause you to experience the wrath of God.

Now, let me shift and define key terms contained in our subject i.e. wisdom and secret. What is wisdom? The Old Testament term *hokmah* denotes wisdom and the term *hakam* refers to being wise. Wisdom has to do with being skillful, experience and shrewdness. In addition, it has to do with having the knowledge, temperament, and ability to make the right choices at the opportune time. In order to ascertain wisdom, there must be a spirit of humility and the willingness to learn what is best because she represents the proven path.

What does the term *secret* mean in scripture? The Old Testament Hebrew word *sod* refers to confidential plan, confidential talk, council, gathering, or circle. The philosophy of secrecy permeates around being disciplined and carrying out a plan (including withholding information) on behalf of a group as opposed to displaying personal interest or selfish gain. Therefore, why are you keeping that secret? God's secrets are wholesome in nature, purpose driven, and preserved in a spiritual incubator until it is appropriate for the righteous to gain access. God's secrets are good and beneficial, and likewise, it is very unlikely for you to stumble upon gold and other precious minerals.

By contrast, many of you think you are smart/wise and withhold information or secrets because your intentions are evil. Ill-advised or inappropriate secrets, whether personal or collective, will eventually be disclosed. Therefore, you need to make sure your secrets are righteous and not devilish. Some of you are wrestling with information you need to reveal while some of you are disclosing information you should keep to yourself.

Knowing when to speak or reveal something as opposed to keeping it a secret remains an interesting topic. This reminds me of the story about four monks who decided to keep silent for a month. Therefore, they decided to leave their monastery and go into the mountain. Immediately upon leaving, one of the monks said, "I do not believe I locked my room." Another monk responded by saying, "We are not supposed to be talking." The third Monk, said, "Well, how about you?" Finally, the last Monk said, "Thank God, I am the only one who hasn't said anything."

No one in his or her right mind wants to feel abandoned and taken advantage. However, it takes disheartening moments and disappointments to propel or position us to enter the secret place. Therefore, if you are truly interested in embracing a fulfilled life, then let me suggest three steps you need to take, so that hereafter you will clearly know what is meant by wisdom and the secret place.

1. Now, the first thing you need to do is open your heart and ears to the discovery of truth by means of remembering the diligent efforts it takes to gain access to gold and the precious minerals in the earth, so that you will begin to lay a foundation for wisdom and the secret place. Putting it another way, the truth and meaningful things in life are always there because they are actual, persistent, and disclosed only after you have put forth a sincere effort.

2. The second thing you need to do is to sanctify and cleanse your heart from the filth and residue associated with the inherent quality of the product in terms of remembering how gold and silver is washed in the water and then taken through the refining fire in order to appreciate the beauty expressed in the finished product all because noteworthy products must be tested by the water and fire.

3. The third and final point has to do with the esteemed value or distinct quality of the finished product, by means of seeing yourself as an over-corner or precious jewel shaped by the hands of the Master Craftsman of life, so that those around me will marvel and admire the quality of my existence in this world.

I have been blessed to observe firsthand the manner in which gold dust is transformed into gold bars. Initially, the gold is not shining and attractive. Nonetheless, the skillful eyes of the goldsmith authorize him to determine the true value. Therefore, he places it in a container and allows the fire to test it in order to determine its worth in carats. Earlier, I mentioned the role of the shaft during the process of collecting the gold because it is a reminder there will always be an outlet, even in the darkened places of your life.

I have entered into the darkened, murky, and lonely tunnel that is often paved with fear and doubt, but I have discovered something new and wonderful beyond the unattractive sights. I have learned truth and falsehood appear, together. Brass can shine like gold, but you know the difference upon testing. A hypocrite can impress you for a while because they behave life a saint. However, you will know who is faking and who is for real once the fire is turned up and the challenges come.

Do you really want to escape from the falcon in the sky and the beast on the ground? Are you tired of playing church and being entangled with frivolous concerns? God is waiting beneath the surface of all the stuff you had to go through and escort you into the secret place of worship and praise.

Let me close with two short stories because the

signs and information will be there, but you must overcome stupidity. A garage mechanic answered the distress call of a stranded motorist whose car had stalled. He responded to the call and made an examination. "Your car is out of gas," he stated.

"Will it hurt the car," asked the distressed motorist, "if I drive it home with the gas tank empty?"

Or

One evening, an old, Cherokee Indian told his grandson about a battle that goes on inside of people. He said, "My son, the battle is between two wolves inside us all."

"One is evil. It is angry, envy, jealousy, sorrow, regret, greed, arrogance, self-pity, guilt, resentment, inferiority, lies, false pride, superiority, and ego. The other is good- It is joy, peace, love, hope, serenity, humility, kindness, benevolence, empathy, generosity, truth, compassion, and faith." The grandson thought about it for a minute, and then asked his grandfather "which wolf wins?" The old Cherokee simply replied, "The one you feed." There is joy and fulfillment in discovering the ultimate treasure, wisdom. God bless.

Job's Summary Defense (Chapters 29-31)

The sermon gave us more insights into the text regarding the nature of God and the human quest for guidance and fulfillment. In this chapter, we will observe Job longing to be in a place from past experiences wherein he sensed the favor and presence of God upon his life. Verse 4 gives us a true sense of what he is missing: friendship of God.

Verse 7 continues the longing; however, there is a shift, wherein he also misses the respect he experienced by youth and nobility. He continued making reference to the testimony of assisting the disinherited. He took great pride in championing the cause of those in dire need.

He wraps this section up by longing for the days when men listen, not accuse as his friends are doing. Once, Job had spoken the wisdom and integrity channeled through him without any additional remarks. However, times and conditions have reversed, and he is displayed in these realities and more.

Chapter 30 expounds upon Job's defense by drawing a contrast between his illustrious past and his current, shameful circumstances. Job envisioned the way he is publicly displayed as the younger disrespectful, peers pass judgment, and he is the spectacle of life.

Verse 11 utilized the loose cord as a descriptive way of saying God has allowed people at random to seize his property, including his tent. Verses 16-23 shows him shifting from the manner by which he is perceived by others and the things they are doing to that of languishing in loneliness and despair, even death.

The remaining verses give further details of a helpless man. He is reminding God and friends of how he assisted those who were in his predicament. However, it appears God, friends, and the people have abandoned him, as expressed in verse 27.

Chapter 31 gives us Job's final appeal. The

previous chapters defended his integrity before God and man. In this chapter, we see an array of hope and optimism, once again. He draws a parallel: if he has been unrighteous, where is the proof? If he has been righteous, where is the favor? Therefore, he requested in the court of life to be weighed in a just balance.

In so doing, he moved from the general to the specific. For example, he asked his wife to step forward and say if he has been unfaithful. This statement gives us the inclination to believe she was yet around. He goes on asking the poor and servants to testify. He suggests even gold and status cannot claim he has been unfair. Job requested his haters, travelers, or anyone who can prove dishonesty to step forward. Job ended his discourse convinced he has been truthful to God and humanity yet could not put a handle on his circumstances.

The lingering questions remain throughout all generations. Namely, why do the righteous suffer and how do we handle suffering while undergoing accusation?

Elihu Speaks on Various Topics (Chapters 32-37)

From the opening chapter, he is not mentioned in the circle of friends associated with Job, but in order for Elihu to have this access, proximity, and opportunity to speak at length, then he is also a friend. He is much younger, but rest assured he has as much, if not more than the other three friends had done earlier, to say. Who is this guy, and where did he come from? Answering these and other questions will help explain how people gain access to you and say a whole lot about life and you that (for the most part could have been kept) was unnecessary. Nonetheless, like Job, you must also hear it, anyhow.

It is always important and helpful to identify and establish biblical characters, especially when they play a significant role. Elihu is identified through ancestral lineage in chapter 32:2. His name denotes, *He is my God himself.* He is a descendant of the Buzite (Genesis 22:20-21), thus identifying him as a nephew of Abraham. I find it interesting to note Job comes from Uz (Genesis 10:21-31) and is associated with Abraham. Moreover, Buz is similar to Uz, wherein both are associated with Abraham. He is also referred to as the forefather of the Tribe of Judah or Davidic Line (1 Chronicle 27:18 & 1 Samuel 1:1). Once again, you can clearly see the African Hebrew Israelite connection. Furthermore, you can clearly see the story of Job and friends can be historically, geographically, and culturally identified.

Elihu Rebukes Job's Three Friends (Chapter 32)

After a series of cycles, Elihu waited his turn to shed some light on what is going on. It should also be noted his father (*Barachel*) is suggested to mean *May God bless*. This young man displays a sense of respect and knowing when to speak. Nonetheless, he is disappointed both with Job and his friends (verses 1-5). What was wrong with Job, and why was God not being justified?

Verses 6-22 give us an overview of a youthful speech. His naiveté is acknowledged and so is the wisdom recognized as the virtue of God. Therefore, the aged are not necessarily wise. He claimed to have been patient in order to hear the truth of the matter come forth but to no avail. He goes on to suggest he is full of words, and the spirit of truth flows through him and promises to be impartial (verse 21).

Elihu Rebukes Job (Chapter 33)

In this chapter, Elihu continues and shifts from the general to the specific. He wants Job's full attention as we see in a court of law. He established his integrity by referencing God has caused him to be and do what he is doing.

In verse 5, the interrogation begins as a directive having Job answer him, truthfully. He appears humble and respectful, referencing both are made from clay. He goes on to assure Job he has listened carefully to his righteous claim. However, he disagrees and begins explaining in verse 12. In other words, Job is not right.

He attempts to explain how God behaves via one or two ways. Furthermore, God utilizes dreams, visions, and opens the ears to hear.

Verses 19-28 seem to suggest Job was punished but not destroyed as a means of allowing him to repent and be restored (verses 24 & 26).

Even further, he expressed in the latter verses (29-33) God allowed all these misfortunes to occur three times in order to awaken him. He firmly requested Job to justify himself or remain silent as he continued his discourse. Wow!

Elihu Asserts God's Justice (Chapter 34)

This is truly an interesting chapter, and it is similar to his opening statement but much more detailed. Once again, the setting is similar to a court room, wherein justice and truth are being pursued. He opens by demanding respect and attention.

His intent is to convince Job and friends what is right to weigh in and pay attention. On one hand, Job claimed to be right, and God has taken away my right (verse 5). Therefore, he sets out to prove Job is wrong and God is right.

Job, he asserts, is being punished for his wrongful deeds because it is not in the nature of God to punish the righteous. God is holy and cannot do wicked and perverted acts. He continues to make this appeal to wise and prudent men (suggesting Job is not one of them). Life and death have consequences similarly to failure show a king respect.

He asserts, God sees and knows all things, including the acts of evildoers. God shifts positions with the unrighteous and righteous without telling anyone what is occurring. What can anyone do when God chooses not to speak? He is confident Job cannot answer, and that supports his position regarding the fate and punishment administered to him. Elihu asserts Job's punishment is compounded because of rebellion and not humility.

Elihu Condemns Job: He Has No Rights (Chapter 35)

This young man is truly on a roll, figuratively speaking. He asked questions and provided the answers. He points out the fault for both Job and his friends. Therefore, he called upon the universe to support his claim and the wisdom he has ascertained. Putting it plainly, he felt Job's claim to righteousness is unsupported just as clouds are far removed from us.

He alludes the proud and arrogant plead for justice when they are in trouble. He wants to know where the true worshippers that can release a song in the night are. God is not impressed with empty or shallow words, such as Job's. The young man seems to have a lot to say, and in many instances, it is truth. However, the statements are out of context and targeting the righteous: Job. He is outright accusing Job more so than the previous ones. However, in this instance, Job is not responding at all like we saw, earlier. Apparently, Job is getting it. There comes a time when silence is far better than defending oneself with lengthy responses.

Elihu Extols God's Greatness (Chapter 36)

The lecture or discourse continues but with a slight twist. In this chapter and the one that follows, God is accredited with giving him the knowledge and foundation of righteousness.

The greatness and sovereignty of the Almighty is laid out. For example, the righteous are remembered while the wicked is alienated. He re-affirms a prevailing thought by suggesting the cords of the affliction are punished. However, if the same shows remorse and contrition, God will show mercy. For him, God has been speaking, but Job is not listening.

The suggestion and implication is made, wherein judgment has come upon Job based upon his ungodly behavior. The term *ransom* is mentioned as a means of reminding Job a tremendous loss or price has already been paid. God is always teaching, but iniquity separates us from God's favor. The remaining verses draws upon various colorful ways of depicting the great and detailed manner for how God operates in Creation, such as the rain, clouds, lightning, sea, judging people, food, and livestock etc.

Elihu Proclaims God's Majesty (Chapter 37)

Now, we come to the final chapter pertaining to Elihu's comments. God speaks emphatically such as thunder and lightning getting our attention. Therefore, Job and all creation should listen to the voice of God.

The details and in-depth manner of God is continued by alluding to the snow, beasts, wind, ice, correction, and love etc. Perhaps he felt Job was not fully paying attention or he simply sense a fresh revelation, he said, "Hear this, O Job." In essence he tells Job God makes no mistakes and no one can compare or come close to doing what He does.

He wraps this chapter up by referencing the light appearing after the storm or darkness. A cardinal flying north is mentioned, and so is the majesty of God. Lastly, God is hidden and mysterious yet fair and honest in all His ways. Deceit and falsehood automatically ushers in the disfavor of God.

The Lord Answers Job (Chapters 38:1-42:2)

Interestingly, God does not speak to any of the four men who have accused and lectured Job. Instead, the Almighty speaks to the one who truly matters: Job. Life is full of nonsense, and sooner or later the unnecessary talk will cease. Unlike, Elihu God is authorized to ask questions, point out hidden things, rebuke yet rebuild character.

The whirlwind is mentioned again because this serves as an attention grabber. Once again, we see a court setting but in the highest dimension. True to form, a profound lawyer or experienced Judge will ask a series of questions. Instead of judgment due to transgression we are about to witness a series of enlightening questions clearly designed to rebuild and undergird Job, the accused.

Knowledge is often hidden such as described in darkened counsel. Job is called upon to take the stand in the presence of the Lord as God interrogates him. This session will recapture all of the ill-informed statements previously made or assumptions Job presumed.

The chapter is a classic. Job is asked where he was when the blueprint and implementation of the earth took place. Where were you when the *Sons of God* worshipped and praised God? Job is questioned regarding the climate, geography, earth's measurement, war and peace, rain and desolation, etc.

The question goes deeper by asking him to identify and explain the members of the constellation. Can Job's voice be heard in the clouds? Once again, lightning and wisdom are testimonies of God's power. God's provision is noted for the beast and raven.

Chapter 39: Animals have always been interesting topics biblically and universally speaking when it comes to wisdom and truth. God points out to Job the nature or purpose for the following animals: mountain goats, donkey, wild ox, ostrich, horse, locust, hawk, and eagle. All in all, eight animals are mentioned, and perhaps this suggests a new beginning is unfolding for Job. Job is unable or not permitted to speak although the questions and analogies are pouring out. Herein, lies a great lesson for each of us. Sometimes in life, we simply cannot and should not attempt to answer the unanswerable but rather remain resolved in our faith until the appropriate answer surfaces.

Chapter 40: The lecture or shall we say admonition from the Lord continues in this chapter. A *faultfinder* (an attention grabber) is utilized in order to get Job's attention. A faultfinder is someone who habitually finds faults, complaints, or objects, especially in petty ways. Therefore, Job is cautioned and challenged to answer and consider all God has to say regarding his behavior and demeanor.

Apparently, God has gotten his attention, whereby he acknowledged speaking immaturely or inappropriately in the past (verses 4-5). This gesture, hand over mouth, is a demonstration of humility and submission to God.

The remaining verses from 6-24 through the next chapter continue disclosing the Lord's challenge to Job. Once again, the whirlwind is utilized to get Job's attention regarding what is truly going on in his life. God will interrogate and Job is asked to respond, if he can.

Samples of the questions and statements uttered by God are listed, below:

- ➢ Can God be condemned and you right?
- ➢ What happens to the proud versus the humble?
- ➢ Take note of *Behemoth* and the provision made for him in his habitat. In some instances, it is referred to as cattle or hippopotami.
- ➢ The same is likened to power, cedar, bronze, and iron

- The lotus plant represents beauty, majesty, tranquility and peace
- Lastly, no person can simply walk up to a hippo and do as they please, such as with the eye and nose.

Despite all these scenarios depicting the sovereignty of God throughout nature, Job remains silent or unable to adequately respond. Apparently, he is learning when and when not to speak.

Chapter 41: This chapter captures our attention by introducing another creature from antiquity known as *Leviathan*, suggested to be the crocodile. The hippo is the most powerful in the rivers of the savannah followed by the crocodile. He is revered and cannot be easily domesticated. Verses 1-8 give us several analogies regarding this creature and man. However, it is quite clear man is no match for this creature.

Verse 9 captures the essence of this scenario. No man in his right mind would attempt to stir up or lay hands on this creature. Verse 12 and the following describe other characteristics of this creature such as his teeth, nostrils, mouth, neck, and heart, etc. He is the epitome of strength and majesty. Plus, mere clubs, javelins, and arrows are no match for him. He is called king over all of the sons of pride.

Chapter 42: Job's Confession and Repentance (verses 1-6)

This chapter will unfold in three parts which depicts resurrection and rebirth. In this section, Job acknowledged his short-comings and realized the eternal plan and compassionate nature of God. Yes, wise counsel is often hidden but attainable through patience, humility, and observation. Job's eyes are truly opened thus preparing him to see what else is about to unfold.

The Lord Rebukes Job's Friends (verses 7-9)

Now, we come to a crucial part in this saga. Job's three friends are about to be rebuked by the Lord. Interestingly, the young man, Elihu is not mentioned. Perhaps this is an indication as to how we behave before our children because after all they are the product of his or her socialization and orientation.

Nonetheless, Eliphaz (first to speak and presumed to be the eldest) is singled out. However, the message is applicable to all three. In essence, God told them they misrepresented him when addressing Job in these matters. Therefore, they are given a mandate to offer a burnt offering sacrifice for their trespasses. Moreover, the one they accused (Job) must pray for them because they are unaligned with God. Take note of their obedience and Job's willingness to forgive and act, accordingly. Talking is finished!

The Lord Restores Job's Fortunes (verses 10-17)

The lessons of life can be prolonged and painful, but you can endure with God. Job was blessed bountifully in the end, including the compassion to pray for his friends to be restored. He received twice as much as he had before. His status in the family and community was restored.

The blessings continued by describing the blessings in properties such as, sheep, camels, oxen, and donkeys. Seven children were born. Of course, we speculate was this the same wife or a new wife. Nonetheless, the focus is on a restored man, Job. The three daughters are given special status in scripture by giving each of their names, *Jemimah* (dove*), Keziah* (perfume) and *Karren-happuch* (eye shadow). In addition, to the daughter's status they were given an inheritance along with the brothers. Job lived 140 years after all these blessings thus supporting the biblical theme of longevity on the earth.

Closing Remarks

The life and legacy of Job is truly universal. The story gives us insights regarding suffering, especially how and how not to behave when suffering comes. The story highlights and diffuses many traditional views that are not necessarily spiritually and theologically sound. For example, suffering is not necessarily the result of sin; sometimes, our closest friends can speak out or term for an extended period; when words are inadequate regarding reality, we must learn to trust silence; women are entitled to inheritance; forgiveness is essential for all parties involved if we want to experience wholeness, and blessings are spiritual in nature but will also eventually include manifestation of things.

The discussion regarding Job transcends geography and ethnicity. He is the depiction of life with multiple faces. I can assure you upon taking subsequent journeys through the book, new revelations and comments will emerge.   Therefore, remain humble before the Lord because God alone knows the heart while men and women are speculating and giving commentaries.

Now, we prepare our heart and soul for the longest scriptural journey in the bible, Psalms. I can assure you this book will truly teach you how to worship and praise God regardless of the circumstances. God bless.

Introduction to Psalms

The Book of Psalms is the longest and most widely read book in the entire Bible. Once again, I will reiterate the English Standard Version is one of my primary sources regarding the layout and basic information throughout these biblical studies.

In all of the previous and subsequent books, we have provided a basic outline highlighting the various chapters and themes. However in this instance, due to a large volume we will take a different route introducing this awesome and diverse compilation. For example, on page 941, ESV we find the structure of the Book of Psalms. I will utilize this as our base and modify accordingly. The Psalms is modeled after the Torah, thus giving us five distinct books.

Books	Scriptures	Comments
Book 1	Psalm 1-41	Psalm 1 & 2 serve as an introduction; however, there is no reference regarding the authorship. The remainder of this book (except for Psalms 10) is accredited to King David. This collection will address distress, ethics, worship, and integrity.

Books	Scriptures	Comments
Book 2	Psalm 42-72	This book introduces the Korah Collections and one Asaph Psalm. David's Psalm resurfaces (51-65; 68-69). In addition, there are Lament and Royal Psalms attributed to King Solomon (72).
Book 3	Psalm 73-89	There is a shift in the tone, wherein the initial Psalm questions the justice of God but eventually acknowledges the great light. This section gives us most of Asap and Korah Psalms (73-88).

Books	Scriptures	Comments
Book 4	Psalm 90-106	It appears the opening Psalm addressed the concerns discussed in book 3.
Book 5	Psalm 107-150	It appears this book accentuates the closing petition in Book 4 because it emphasized God answers prayer. There are five distinct Hallelujah Psalms (106-150). The longest Psalm (119) and a series of Pilgrimage Psalms refer to Jerusalem (120-134). Psalm 118:8 is considered to be the middle verse in the entire Bible.

Several terms are listed below that will assist you throughout your journey of praise and worship and a well-preserved, ageless book:

Terms	Explanation	Text
Image	A word or phrase that names a concrete action or thing by an extension, a character, setting, or event in story is an image (A concrete embodiment of human experience/idea).	Psalm 1 way (path) congregation (assembly)
Metaphor	An implied comparison and figure of speech that describes a subject by asserting it is the same on some point of comparison as another unrelated object. It does not use the formula *like* or *as*.	Psalm 23:1

Terms	Explanation	Text
Simile	A figure of speech in which a writer compares two things using the formula *like* and *as*.	Psalm 1:3
Personification	A figure of speech in which human attributes are given to something nonhuman such as animals, objects, or abstract qualities.	Psalm 43:3 light & truth
Hyperbole	A figure of speech in which a writer consciously exaggerates for the sake of effect and conveying truth.	Psalm 42:3

Terms	Explanation	Text
Apostrophe	A figure of speech in which the writer addresses a person's absence as though they are present and capable of responding.	Psalm 148:3

Types or Categories of Psalms

> **Laments**: The writer presents a troubled situation before the Lord and petitions Him for assistance. There are both individual and communal laments. The term *lament* is often associated with crying and anguish. Lament Psalms are the largest compilation.

> **Hymns of Praise**: The writer invites or summons the covenant community to admire the wonderful deeds and attributes of God on their behalf.

> **Hymns of Thanksgiving**: The writer creates a scenario, wherein God has responded favorably to a petition; therefore, the community is called upon to express their gratitude.

> **Hymns Celebrating God's Law**: The Torah was revealed to Moses, wherein present and future generations might know and understand the spiritual and ethical mandates assigned to Israel and all nations that adhere to holiness.

> **Wisdom Psalms**: Psalm is placed in the Wisdom Literature. Therefore, it stands to reason to have

Psalms serving as a reminder what is the proven path for wisdom.

➤ **Songs of Confidence:** Trust and reliance on Yahweh is paramount. Therefore, Psalms 23 serves as a model for reminding the faith community to be mindful.

➤ **Royal Psalms:** The Davidic Dynasty served as the spiritual blueprint and archetype for the Messiah. So, from time to time elaborate and regal festivals were initiated as a means of thanking God.

➤ **Historical Psalms:** It is always appropriate to recount past experiences, good and bad. Afterward, designated memorials and activities should be put in place to praise and thank God for grace and mercies.

➤ **Prophetic Hymns:** The prophetic voice operates in the Messianic Kingdom. Therefore, the voice of the prophet serves as a vivid reminder for Israel to remain faithful and distinct as a Holy Nation.

I also want to introduce you to a prevailing literary term and style that is consistent throughout the entire book, *Parallelism.* This term refers to using elements in sentences that are grammatically similar or identical in structure, sound, meaning, or meter. This technique adds symmetry, effectiveness, and balance to the written piece.

Contemporary and scriptural examples of parallelism are listed in order to enlighten or assist you on this spiritual journey:

You need to work, quickly and decisively.

He was a prolific author: writing poems, short stories, novels, and screenplays.

Like father, like son.

This is not only just what I wanted, but also just what I needed.

Easy come, easy go.

What goes around comes around.

I am neither a Catholic nor a Protestant.

The problem was not in planning or in development, but rather in production.

Psalms 1 - Benefits of a blessed man versus one who is not blessed.

Psalms 2:4 - Evil will not prevail under the watchful eyes of God.

Psalms: 42:1 – The soul desires for God.

Psalm 49:1-2 – Give unto the Lord (what, who and why)

Discussions regarding the Psalm are unending. There are additional categories such as Hallel, Ascents, Liturgical, and Individual Psalms, etc. The researcher should note there is also *The Egyptian Hallel Psalms* (113-118). Psalms gives us a rhythmic cadence within and without the covenant community for wholesome living. Israel was summoned by God to praise and worship Him in the midst of cultures and groups who adhered to a different lifestyle. These Psalms will connect with you because there is truth in the axiom *nothing new under the sun.*

Regarding the etymology or origin or the word *Psalm,* it should be noted it is derived from the Hebrew term *Tehillim* denoting Praise. However, the current term is derived from the Greek *Psalmoi* meaning Instrumental Music. Literally speaking, it means word accompanying music. Hopefully, you will gain deeper appreciation for the charisma and soulful manner by which Africans worldwide praise and worship God.

Lastly, in the introduction you should take note that each closing section within the five books closes with a doxology:

➤ "Blessed be the Lord, the God of Israel, from everlasting to…" 41:13 (Book 1)
➤ "Blessed be his glorious name forever; may the whole earth be filled… 72:20 (Book 2)

- ➤ "Blessed be the Lord forever! Amen and Amen." 89:52 (Book 3)
- ➤ "Blessed be the Lord, the God of Israel, from everlasting to everlasting... 106:48 (Book 4)
- ➤ "Let everything that has breath praise the Lord! Praise the Lord! 150:6 (Book 5)

While browsing the Internet searching for new and analytical data regarding the Psalms, I came across a document *Types of Psalms* under www.usefulcharts.com. This chart captures Psalms by giving us an overview of each section or division. Therefore, the cliché, *"Why re-invent the wheel?"* applies to this situation, wherein I will add this as an attachment and supplement to these lectures.

Psalm is vast in content but practical and welcoming throughout each stanza. Generally speaking, the two largest categories of Psalms are, *Lament Psalms* and *Praise Psalms.* For example, there are 58 *Lament Psalms* and 42 *Praise Psalms.* Thus laying claim to 100 of the 150 Psalms. Therefore, I want to share a few remarks on Lament Psalms and Praise Psalms.

Lamenting was and is a common distraught demeanor throughout Africa and Semitic Cultures. Scripturally, there are numerous terms describing this gesture. For introductory purposes the term, *Saphad* denotes wail, mourn and sad etc. Generally speaking a Lament Psalms surfaced during the time of needs, and there are basically four types of Lament Psalms: Corporate; Personal; Repentance and Imprecation (cursing or wishing evil on someone). Listed below are the 5 parts of a Lament Psalm utilizing Psalms 142 as a practical illustration:

1. **Address and Petition** (Verses 1-3a)

2. **The Lament/Real Problem** (verses 3b-4)

3. **Confession & Acknowledgement of Trust** (verse 5)

4. **Prayer Request to God & may include reason for answering prayer** (verse 6)

5. **Vow & Shout of Praise & may include Prophetic Statement** (verse 7)

In addition to the aforementioned format, there is yet another way you may study Lament Psalms. For example, you can utilize these methods: Complaint; Call to God for help; or Confession of Trust

Now, a few remarks regarding Praise Psalms. A Praise Psalm derives from the Hebrew word *Yadah* literally meaning praise both individually, collectively, and publicly. A brief format is listed below:

1. **Call to Praise** (self or others)

2. **Reason for Praise** (attributes of God or deeds of God)

3. **Conclusion** (often repetition of opening verse)

Putting it another way Praise Psalms may be expressed **Declarative** (to make known or explain) **or Descriptive** (noting, concerned with or based upon facts). Throughout the Psalms the covenant community is encouraged to render praise and worship in all circumstances and in so doing this makes them peculiar and unique among the nations.

Assignment: The following exercise comes from Book I of the Psalms:

- ➤ Explain the threefold section displayed in Psalm 1, namely, Verses 1-2; 3-4; and 5-6.
- ➤ Utilize either of the formats listed above then apply to Psalm 7 (Lament).
- ➤ Do the same for Psalm 14.
- ➤ Apply the format listed above for Psalm 8, a Praise Psalm.
- ➤ Do the same for Psalm 29
- ➤ What is the longest Psalm in Book 1?
- ➤ Share your thoughts on the same as a Praise and Wisdom Psalms
- ➤ The 23rd Psalm is a classic and labeled a Trust Psalm. Please describe the twofold scenarios, namely, The Lord as Shepherd and Lord as the Host.

Please submit this assignment in writing to me or email prior to next class. Thank you.

Types of Psalms

There are many different types of psalms, the two main types being **LAMENTS** (prayers in times of need) and songs of **PRAISE** (worship in times of joy). However, there are also: songs of **THANKSGIVING** (for specific instances when God answered prayer), **WISDOM** psalms (designed for teaching), **ROYAL** psalms (written for the king), confessions of **TRUST** (used when facing a specific trial), **TEMPLE** entry liturgies (sung together before entering the temple) and **PILGRIM** songs (sung together on a pilgrimage).

Psalm	Genre	Attributed to:	Notes:	Psalm	Genre	Attributed to:	Notes:
BOOK I - Mostly Davidic psalms with psalms 1 & 2 perhaps being an introduction to the entire collection				19	PRAISE (v1-6) / WISDOM (v7-14)	David	has two main parts; the first speaks of God's revelation in nature and the second speaks of God's revelation through scripture
1	WISDOM	Anonymous		20	ROYAL	David	
2	ROYAL	Anonymous	includes the phrase, "You are my Son; today I have become your Father," (v7) which is quoted several times in the NT in reference to Christ	21	ROYAL	David	
3	LAMENT	David	written when David fled from his son Absalom	22	LAMENT	David	starts with the phrase, "My God, my God, why have thou forsaken me?" (v1) which was quoted by Jesus on the cross
4	LAMENT	David					
5	LAMENT	David		23	TRUST	David	The most famous psalm; starts with, "The Lord is my shephard, I shall not want"
6	LAMENT	David	1st of the 7 penitential psalms				
7	LAMENT	David	psalm of the falsely accused	24	TEMPLE	David	Begins with the phrase, "The earth is the Lord's, and everything in it" (v1)
8	PRAISE	David	begins with, "O Lord, our Lord, how majestic is your name in all the earth!" (v1) and includes the phrase, "what is man that you are mindful of him?" (v4)	25	LAMENT	David	an acrostic
				26	LAMENT	David	
9	LAMENT	David	originally one psalm	27	LAMENT	David	
10	LAMENT	David		28	LAMENT	David	
11	TRUST	David		29	PRAISE	David	
12	LAMENT	David		30	THANKS	David	written for the dedication of the temple
13	LAMENT	David	model lament - includes a complaint (v1-2), a call to God for help (v3-4), and a confession of trust in God's love (v5-6)	31	LAMENT	David	
				32	THANKS	David	2nd of the 7 penitential psalms
14	LAMENT	David	same as psalm 53; includes the phrase, "The fool says in his heart, 'There is no God'" (v1)	33	PRAISE	Anonymous	
				34	THANKS	David	an acrostic; written after David pretended to be insane before Abimelech
15	TEMPLE	David	starts with the questions, "Lord, who may dwell in your sanctuary? Who may live on your holy hill?" (v1)	35	LAMENT	David	
				36	LAMENT	David	
16	TRUST	David		37	WISDOM	David	an acrostic; written after David pretended to be insane before Abimelech
17	LAMENT	David					
18	ROYAL	David	written when David was delivered from Saul; also recorded in 2 Samuel 22; includes the phrase, "The Lord is my rock, my fortress, and my deliverer" (v2)	38	LAMENT	David	3rd of the 7 penitential psalms
				39	LAMENT	David	
				40	THANKS	David	v13-17 repeated in psalm 70
				41	LAMENT	David	a psalm about illness; v14 is a doxology (ending) to Book I

Psalm	Genre	Attributed to:	Notes:	Psalm	Genre	Attributed to:	Notes:
BOOK II - Start of the Elohistic psalms (until 83); these psalms tend to use the word Elohim for God instead of Yahweh; most are attributed to the Korahites or David				69	PRAISE	David	
				70	LAMENT	David	a repeat of psalm 40:13-17
42	LAMENT	Korahites	originally one psalm; begins with, "As the deer pants for streams of water, so my soul pants for you, O God" (v1)	71	LAMENT	Anonymous	
43	LAMENT	Korahites		72	ROYAL	Solomon	one of only two psalms attributed to King Solomon; v18-19 is a doxology (ending) to Book II
44	LAMENT	Korahites					
45	ROYAL	Korahites	a wedding song	BOOK III - a collection of psalms, most of which are attributed to Asaph or the Korahites			
46	PRAISE	Korahites	a song of Zion; includes the phrase, "Be still and know that I am God" (v10)	73	WISDOM	Asaph	
47	PRAISE	Korahites	a song of Yahweh's kingship	74	LAMENT	Asaph	
48	PRAISE	Korahites	a song of Zion	75	THANKS	Asaph	
49	WISDOM	Korahites		76	PRAISE	Asaph	a song of Zion
50	Prophetic Oracle	Asaph		77	LAMENT	Asaph	
				78	WISDOM	Asaph	
51	LAMENT	David	written after the prophet Nathan came to David after David had committed adultery with Bathsheba; 4th of the 7 penitential psalms	79	LAMENT	Asaph	
				80	LAMENT	Asaph	
52	LAMENT	David	written after the high priest Ahimelech had been executed by Saul for helping David (see 1 Samuel 22)	81	PRAISE	Asaph	
				82	LAMENT	Asaph	
53	LAMENT	David	a repeat of psalm 14	83	LAMENT	Asaph	
54	LAMENT	David	written when David was hiding from Saul	84	PRAISE	Korahites	a song of Zion
55	LAMENT	David		85	LAMENT	Korahites	
56	LAMENT	David	written when David was captured by the Philistines	86	LAMENT	David	
57	LAMENT	David	written when David was hiding from Saul in a cave	87	PRAISE	Korahites	a song of Zion
58	LAMENT	David		88	LAMENT	Korahites; Heman the Ezrahite	
59	LAMENT	David	written when Saul had sent men to watch David's house in order to kill him	89	ROYAL	Ethan the Ezrahite	v53 is a doxology (ending) to Book III
60	LAMENT	David	written after a major military defeat	BOOK IV - a collection of mostly anonymous psalms			
61	LAMENT	David		90	LAMENT	Anonymous	only psalm attributed to Moses
62	TRUST	David		91	TRUST	Anonymous	
63	TRUST	David		92	PRAISE	Anonymous	
64	LAMENT	David		93	PRAISE	Anonymous	a song of Yahweh's kingship
65	PRAISE	David		94	LAMENT	Anonymous	
66	PRAISE	Anonymous		95	PRAISE	Anonymous	
67	PRAISE	Anonymous		96	PRAISE	Anonymous	a song of Yahweh's kingship
68	PRAISE	David		97	PRAISE	Anonymous	a song of Yahweh's kingship
				98	PRAISE	Anonymous	a song of Yahweh's kingship

70

Psalm	Genre	Attributed to:	Notes:
99	PRAISE	Anonymous	a song of Yahweh's kingship
100	PRAISE	Anonymous	
101	ROYAL	David	
102	LAMENT	David	5th of the 7 penitential psalms
103	PRAISE	Anonymous	
104	PRAISE	Anonymous	
105	PRAISE	Anonymous	
106	PRAISE	Anonymous	v48 is a doxology (ending) to Book IV
BOOK V - mostly anonymous psalms with 146-150 being a conclusion to the entire Book of Psalms			
107	THANKS	Anonymous	
108	PRAISE	David	
109	LAMENT	David	
110	ROYAL	David	
111	PRAISE	Anonymous	
112	WISDOM	Anonymous	
113	PRAISE	Anonymous	
114	PRAISE	Anonymous	
115	PRAISE	Anonymous	
116	THANKS	Anonymous	
117	PRAISE	Anonymous	The shortest psalm and shortest chapter in the Bible (only two verses)
118	THANKS	Anonymous	includes the phrase, "This is the day the LORD has made; let us rejoice and be glad in it." (v24)
119	WISDOM	Anonymous	an acrostic; the longest psalm and longest chapter in the Bible (176 verses)

The Egyptian Hallel - Passover sung during

Psalm	Genre	Attributed to:	Notes:
120	PILGRIM	Anonymous	
121	PILGRIM	Anonymous	beings with the phrase, "I lift up my eyes to the hills" (v1)
122	PILGRIM	David	
123	PILGRIM	Anonymous	
124	PILGRIM	David	
125	PILGRIM	Anonymous	
126	PILGRIM	Anonymous	
127	PILGRIM	Solomon	beings with the phrase, "Unless the Lord builds the house" (v1)
128	PILGRIM	Anonymous	
129	PILGRIM	Anonymous	
130	PILGRIM	Anonymous	6th of the 7 penitential psalms
131	PILGRIM	David	
132	PILGRIM	Anonymous	a song of Zion
133	PILGRIM	David	begins with the phrase, "How good and pleasant it is when brothers live together in unity!" (v1)
134	PILGRIM	Anonymous	
135	PRAISE	Anonymous	
136	PRAISE	Anonymous	known as "The Great Hallel"; has 26 lines, each of which ends with the phrase, "for his mercy endureth for ever"
137	LAMENT	Anonymous	basis for the Boney M song "By the Rivers of Babylon"
138	PRAISE	David	
139	LAMENT	David	
140	LAMENT	David	
141	LAMENT	David	
142	LAMENT	David	
143	LAMENT	David	7th of the 7 penitential psalms
144	ROYAL	David	
145	PRAISE	David	
146	PRAISE	Anonymous	
147	PRAISE	Anonymous	
148	PRAISE	Anonymous	
149	PRAISE	Anonymous	
150	PRAISE	Anonymous	

Songs of Ascent - sung during the journey to Jerusalem for festivals

Find more great charts at
www.usefulcharts.com

71

Psalm Book I: Assignment Answers

1. Explain the following sections in Psalm 1:

   - (Verses 1-2)   The writer presents a parallel or contrast reference to values and source. The choice is yours, adhere and submit to a life of righteousness or succumb to the failures of unrighteousness.
   - (Verses 3-4) These scriptures give us another comparison regarding the results or fruits in life by utilizing similes (tree and water). What results are you experiencing?
   - (Verses 5-6)   These verses shed light on the outcome in this life regarding the judgment based upon the choices you make.

2. Psalm 7 is a Lament Psalm, and the following breakdown supports the Lament format:

   - Petition (verse 1)
   - Problem (verse 2)
   - Confession (verse 3)
   - Prayer (verses 3-16)
   - Vow (verse 17)

3. Psalm 14 is another Lament Psalm, and the following is the other format:

   - Complaint (verses 1-2)
   - Call to God (verses 3-6)
   - Confession (verse 7)

4. Psalm 7 is a Praise Psalm, and the following is the Praise format:

- Call to praise (verses1-2)
- Reason for praise (verses 3-8)
- Conclusion (verse 9)

5. Psalm 29 is a Praise Psalm, and the following is the Praise format:

- Call to praise (verses 1-2)
- Reason for praise (verses 3-10)
- Conclusion (verse 11)

6. The longest Psalms in Book 1 is Psalm 18. It consists of fifty verses.

7. Psalm 18 may be classified as a Royal, Wisdom, and Praise Psalm. Overall, the psalmist highlights the goodness and faithfulness of Yahweh on behalf of Israel. In order to amplify this claim, he utilized various scenes of nature.

8. Psalm 23 is presented in two parts, namely *The Lord is a Good Shepherd* (verses 1-4) and *The Lord is a Gracious Host* (verses 5-6). All in all, God looks after and makes all the provisions for the covenant community, Israel.

Psalm Book II

Book II (42-72) is the third longest (Book 5 is the longest). Let me take a moment and introduce or peak your interest by describing the Korahites because these Psalms are noted at least eight times in this book.

The **Korites** are descendants of Aaron the brother of Moses and first High Priest of Israel. Numbers chapter three introduces them as Levites and their roles. Specifically, they were commissioned to take care of the Tabernacle, including the Ark of Covenant.

I do not shun from the truth that the Bible is fundamentally the story of Africans from diverse culture. There is a tradition that suggests and connects the Maasai Tribe in Kenya and Tanzania with the Korahites based upon the protective and caretaker lifestyle. Scriptural reference associated with Priest Jedaiah and Meshallum (1 Chronicles 9:10, 12, mentions Maasai and 17).

Levi sons were, Gershon, Merari and Kohath. Korah is the grandson of Kohath (see Numbers 16). They are mentioned throughout Samuel and King David's reign. Therefore, you can see the contribution of the Psalmist is associated with their historical and spiritual role in the covenant community.

The overall intent (hymns of praise) resonates through each Psalm. For example, the Psalmist utilizes scenes of nature, legal jargon, social status, deliverance from trouble, and God's sovereignty etc.

Within this book, Psalm 50 is labeled a **Prophetic Oracle Psalm.** Biblically and universally speaking, an oracle refers to a person or agency authorized to share wise counsel or prophetic predictions for the future inspired by God. The term *oracle* derives from the Latin word *Orare* to speak. Therefore, one can note this Psalm sheds light on the spiritual and ethical expectations and shortfalls within the covenant community.

One should note the following frequently read and discussed Psalms while browsing through this book: 41-42; 46; 51; 53; 55; 62; 68 and 70. It should also be considered each of the book ends with a doxology: "Blessed be his glorious name forever; may the whole earth be filled with his glory! Amen and Amen! (72:20).

I always emphasize the twofold approach to studying the scriptures, namely critical and literal. However, I tend to place emphasis on the critical, simply because Satan has tricked and persuaded far too many to display discipline and resilience when it comes to the Word of God.

The reader should pay attention to how this book ushers a shift in terminology relating to Israel's God. For example, the name Yahweh was prevalent in Book I. Whereas, Psalms 42-83 utilize the name Elohim, and the phrase *Elohistic Psalms* is commonly used. Elohim is the first revealed Hebraic name in scripture (Gen. 1:1-2:4). It basically means creator and judge.

Assignment: The following exercise comes from Book II of the Psalms:

- ➢ Considering David is the prominent author in this book, please comment on 51 Psalms and one more. Afterward, give the historical situation at hand surrounding the Psalm.
- ➢ Given there are only 2 Trust Psalms in this book, what do they tell us?
- ➢ Where is the middle Psalm in this book? What type is it and what is the message?
- ➢ List the longest and shortest Psalm in this book.
- ➢ Identify and expound on your favorite Psalm in this book.
- ➢ Can you tell me who Maskil was in relations to the Korahites?
- ➢ Israel's primary names for her God were, Yahweh and Elohim, please explain?

Psalm Book II: Assignment Answers

1. Psalms 51 is commonly referred as a Penitential Psalm that displays a contrite spirit. King David is believed to be the author, and the Psalms permeates around his bad decision and confession. In other words, David lusted after another man's wife and had him killed. Subsequently, Nathan (the Prophet) is summoned to speak to the king about this matter. For details regarding the origin and parallel of this Psalm, read 2 Samuel 12:1-14.

2. Psalms 62 & 63 are labeled as the only Trust Psalms in Book II, therefore, what are they saying? Psalms 62 clearly portrays the picture of trust and confidence in God as a

rock. In addition, whenever He speaks we should listen, attentively. Psalm 63 makes a similar claim; however, it seems initially to be a Lament Psalms and then shift to depicting our soul's thirsting for spiritual concerns. Despite the attempts of the wicked, our King/God will protect and provide.

3. The middle Psalms in Book II is Psalms 57, a Lament Psalms. More specifically, this seems to be an Individual Lament Psalms, wherein the Psalmist is requesting the mercies of God coupled with God's steadfast love in an environment that otherwise might devour him.

4. The shortest Psalms in Book II is Psalms 43, and the longest Psalms in Book II is Psalms 69.

5. Probably my favorite Psalms in this book is Psalms 51. Of course, Psalms 53 is another favorite. Nonetheless, I will share a few comments in Psalms 51 because this Psalm clearly demonstrates no individual is too big or small to confess when they have transgressed. God is merciful and attentive to the cry of the humble in heart. Therefore, it behooves each of us to make sure the heart and soul remains impeccable.

6. Maskil was a son of Korah who was referenced in Psalms 44, 45, and 52. The term is associated with a Levite and Hebrew Scholar who is also well versed in the sacred writing. This discipline enables the writer to bring together the sacred text and music for authentic praise and worship.

7. Israel in the Bible is introduced as the covenant community in the Old Testament that is summoned by God

with the backdrop of Egypt, Babylon, Chaldea, Kush, and Assyria, etc. The scripture and Hebraic tradition initially identifies these sacred names: *Yahweh* and *Elohim.* The personal name is usually mentioned in scripture in a similar manner as the surrounding kingdoms. The name Yahweh (YHWH) means to be or become and generally denotes LORD. Note the name is generally all capitals in the Bible. On the other hand, Elohim serves as the plural for El (Eloah). This is the first name revealed in scripture Genesis 1:1 and Exodus 3:6. Generally speaking, this term refers to might, power, strength, and creator. Both names are used throughout the Old Testament alongside various attributes of God (16). Even further, the Hebrew term *Dabar* denotes *Word.* Thus, the tri-fold phrase: *Dabar Yahweh Elohim* (Word of Lord God) was created.

Psalm Book III

This book is the shortest of the Psalms, consisting of only sixteen Psalms. Within this book, you will find a variety such as lament, royal, thanks, praise, and wisdom. Once again, we observe by and large Levite Psalms by Asaph and Korah. It is noted the latter was a cousin to Moses and part of a rebellion while in the wilderness (read Numbers 16). The book opens with a Wisdom Psalm and ends with a Community Lament Psalm.

Another way of viewing these Psalms is to consider each as Ritual Psalms. Here is an example how an anonymous person gives a practical illustration of a ritual. "I pound my feet strongly on the ground several times. I take several deep breaths, and I "shake" my body to remove any negative energies. I do this often before going to work, going into meetings and at the front door before entering my house after a long day."

A ritual is a sequence of activities involving a gesture, word, and objects performed in a sequestered place and performed according to a sequence. A ritual is a prescribed order of a religious ceremony. Therefore, Ritual Psalms are words put to music that follows a prescribed pattern. For example, let us examine Psalm 76, a Praise Psalm, but let us review it as a Ritual Psalm that puts forth the profound question: "Who Can Stand before You?

The Psalms establishes a relationship between Yahweh and Judah. Afterward, God defends the faith community despite the onslaught of Israel's experience foes. Verse 7 reiterates the subject, who can stand before you. The Psalm gives a mixture of formats, but in essence we also observe the ritual: God is our source; the people of faith will be challenged; the enemy will be defeated; we will give praise unto God; and our vow and doxology remain in place.

By and large, we have looked at the Psalms from the critical perspective; however, let me share a few comments regarding the literal, devotional, or inspirational means of studying. For example, let me share a few comments from one of the classics, and it is part of the Church of God in Christ Sunday School Devotion (Psalms 84). Your desire for spiritual concerns should ignite a longing and passion for a deeper relationship.

This Psalm is referred to as a Pilgrimage Psalm. It appears Israel is estranged or far removed from Zion or Israel. The temple was designated as the meeting place for worship. Therefore, the heart and soul longs for the sacred place and with great expectance looks forward to returning there. The bird has a place called home, and so does the sons and daughters of the Most High God: Jerusalem.

True worshippers are blessed; therefore, this awareness is accompanied with singing and praises as they enter the sacred place. Meanwhile, they find themselves sojourning through un-inviting and challenging terrain, but the Lord makes provision, even there. There is a reference to one of the patriarch or ancestor. Jacob is a point of reference to the covenant.

Time reference to God accompanied with service on His behalf is far greater than longevity and living outside the grace of God. Yes, trusting in God will cause them to yet experience the blessings although they are not in the preferred place: Jerusalem of God on this pilgrimage. Therefore, praise and worship is appropriate at all times, even when you are not in the preferred place, Jerusalem, trust in God will cause them to yet experience blessings on this pilgrimage. Read the Psalm with a sense of connection as a witness to His glorious ways.

Psalm Book III Assignment

1. Select a Wisdom Psalm from this book and construct your commentary.

2. Select a Lament Psalm from this book and use a format discussed previously.

3. Give me a one line summary for each of the Psalms in this book.

4. Psalm 78, the longest gives us an historical account of Israel. Briefly share your thoughts.

5. Share your comments on the term *parable* in Psalm 78:2 and the New Testament explanation of the same.

6. Some theologians have described Psalms 88 as the bleakest of all Psalms, please explain.

7. Can you compare the overall themes of Asaph Psalms (73-83) and Korah Psalms (84-85 & 87-88)?

8. Which Psalms within this book seem to inspire you the most and explain?

9. Share your thoughts regarding the legal and spiritual understanding in the Bible such as Psalms 75 and 82 etc.

10. Defend the critical and literal approach to the Bible and apply to a selected Psalms in Book III.

Note: Assignment due prior to next class via email or typed copy. Thank you.

Psalm Book IV Assignment

1. Identify the three Lament Psalms and apply a format I shared for one of the Psalm.

2. There are 12 Praise Psalms in this book. Use the format I gave for two of them.

3. Generally speaking, how do you describe the King Psalms?

4. Generally speaking, how do you explain or factor history and environment with Psalms?

5. What is meant by *singing a new song* such as Psalms 97 & 98?

6. Please share your commentaries on Psalm 99.

7. What are the perquisites for making a joyful noise?

8. Psalms 102 describes someone afflicted and crying out to the Lord. Please explain.

9. Psalms 103 & 104 starts off with *"Bless the Lord, O my soul."* Please explain.

10. Psalms 105 & 106 start off with *"Oh give thanks unto the Lord."* Please explain.

11. In your own words, please explain what seems to be the prevailing theme in this book?

Psalm Book IV

This book is unique and has her own personality in that the majority of these Psalms comes from anonymous sources, with the exception of a reference to Moses' (90) and David's (101 & 103) authorship. Altogether, Book IV consists of seventeen Psalms. By and large they serve as a template for praise and public worship.

In line with the Torah, this section relates to the book of Numbers. For example, Numbers describes the emergence of a kingdom: Israel as they were called, *Children of Israel* in relation to her more established neighbors, Egypt, Kush, Canaan, and Assyria etc. In addition, this book makes reference to activities subsequent to the Davidic Kingdom. In other words, God was always in control and guiding Israel and deserved praise and worship at all times.

This book uniquely utilized one of the sacred the names used for God: Yahweh/Jehovah (LORD). However, this is not to say the name Elohim (God) is not used on occasions.

The introduction to the section declares confidence in God as "Protector of His people (90)". The theme of this section is about the steadfastness and faithfulness of God. The doxology or ending Psalm (106) praises God for the way He has led Israel until the present day and declares that He never changes; He is "from everlasting to everlasting". This time, the doxology closes with *Amen* and *Hallelujah* (Praise the Lord)."

Psalm 90 is often accredited to Moses and is labeled a Community Lament Psalm. Nonetheless, the Psalmist recounts Israel's history and her unique relationship with Yahweh. The dwelling place is uniquely identified as a spiritual being, not as a physical place, and this awareness serves as a benchmark and eyeopener. The brevity of life (70 years) is described and often misunderstood in the scripture. The writer goes on to request wisdom (verse 12), whereby prudent decisions can be made through his life. It concluded by appealing for the favor (grace) of God to undergird them throughout their sojourn. Psalms 105-106 are other illustrations recounting history.

The following (Psalm 91) expands the subject, dwelling in reference to Israel place of abode. Israel finds protection and guidance within the shelter of the Lord. Therefore, the Psalmist crafts convincing metaphorical and symbolic expressions based upon Israel's relationship with the Lord.

This book gives us a series of Kingship Psalms highlighting the sovereignty and majesty of Israel's true king: Yahweh/Elohim such as Psalms 93, 96, 97, 98, 99, and 100. Within this framework, Psalm 100 is another classic that is utilized during gospel concerts and when there is an emphasis on praise.

Obviously, Israel is encouraged to praise and exalt Yahweh, but we also note the gentile nations are encouraged to do likewise. The basis for praise and thanksgiving permeates around the goodness, steadfast love, and faithfulness throughout all generations. Creativity coupled with awareness will cause the true believer to praise God anyhow!

Psalms 104 is another favorite Psalm denoting "Bless the Lord…" The righteous are able to return the same spirit of well-being and wholesomeness to God simply because they are able to distinguish fate and destiny. Putting it another way, God is Israel's source and no circumstances or reality can impede His eternal plan for them. "Praise his holy name."

Psalm Book V

This book is the longest and presents us with a variety of Psalms. We will soon observe this compilation concludes in an insightful and inspirational manner. Perhaps, it will be beneficial to give an overview of each Psalms.

Psalm 107: The community is summoned to come together and render praise and thanks to the Lord because of His steadfast love. Meanwhile, they are mindful of various experiences.

Psalm 108: Attributed to King David as a Community Lament that also reflects on various acts of salvation on behalf of Israel.

Psalm 109: An Individual Lament highlighting a situation wherein only God can resolve.

Psalm 110: A Royal Psalm attributed to King David's dynasty, including the Messiah.

Psalm 111: A hymn of praise denoting the Lord's faithfulness.

Psalm 112: One of my favorites denoting the relationship between God and the righteous.

Psalm 113: God's ways are peculiar, including providential care for all. It is also suggested 113-118 are called *Egyptian Hallel Psalms* due to the association with barren women and the Passover.

Psalm 114: A vivid reminder of a covenant and status between Yahweh and Israel.

Psalm 115: Trust and total allegiance to God and no tolerance in idolatry.

Psalm 116: A personal testimony of praise and gratitude to God

Psalm 117: Shortest Psalm but vivid reminder who God is within Israel.

Psalm 118: This concludes the Egyptian Hallel Psalms in the spirit of thanksgiving. In addition, verse 8 is referred as the central verse in the entire Bible

Psalm 119: Not only is this the longest Psalms but it also serves as the longest scripture in the entire Bible, consisting of 176 verses. The writer captures the importance and sacredness of the Torah (spiritual instruction) in a unique and memorable fashion. For example, the Hebrew Alphabets (22) are utilized wherein eight verses are carefully placed beneath each of them. In addition, the writer utilized canon, legal or judicial terms within the context of the spiritual mandates. The terms are noted as testimonies ('edot), laws (torah), precepts (piqqudim), commandments (mitswot), statues (khuggot), rules (mishpatim) and word (totaling 7). You will observe the alphabets are capitalized in a similar manner like the term LORD and YAHWEH throughout the Psalms. Listed below you will observe the breakdown of the alphabets and verses:

1. ALEPH – Verses 1-8

2. BETH – Verses 9-16 (noted verse, "I have stored your word in my heart…")

3. GIMEL – Verses 17-24

4. DALETH – Verses 25-32

5. HE – Verses 33-40

6. WAW – Verses 41-48

7. ZAYIN – Verses 49-56

8. HETH – Verses 57-64

9. TETH – Verses 65-72

10. YODH – Verses 73-80

11. KAPH – Verses 81-88

12. LAMEDH – Verses 89-96

13. MEM – Verses 97-104

14. NUN – Verses 105-12 (contains classic verse, "Your word is a lamp to my feet…")

15. SAMEKH – Verses 113-120

16. AYIN – Verses 121-128 (Hebrew term for eye is Ayin and the same is noted in verse 123).

17. PE – Verses 129-136

18. TSADHE – Verses 137-144

19. QOPH – Verses 145-152

20. RESH – Verses 153-160

21. SIN AND SHIN – Verses 161-168

22. TAW – Verses 169-176

In order to help you understand this ancient style of writing, abstracts from the website www.jewfaq.org (Judaism 101) are listed below.

Hebrew Alphabet

Level: Basic

• Hebrew uses a different alphabet than English
• Hebrew is written right-to-left
• The Hebrew alphabet has no vowels, but pronunciation aids are often added
• There are several styles of Hebrew writing
• Hebrew letters have numerical values
• Writing in Hebrew may require a special word processor and fonts

The Hebrew and Yiddish languages use a different alphabet than English. The picture below illustrates the Hebrew alphabet, in Hebrew alphabetical order. Note that Hebrew is written from right to left, rather than left to right as in English, so Alef is the first letter of the Hebrew alphabet and Tav is the last. The Hebrew alphabet is often called the "alefbet," because of its first two letters.

Letters of the Alefbet

Teit	Cheit	Zayin	Vav	Hei	Dalet	Gimel	Beit	Alef
מ ט	ח	ז	ו	ה	ד	ג	ב	א
(T)	(Ch)	(Z)	(V/O/U)	(H)	(D)	(G)	(B/V)	(Silent)

Samekh	Nun	Nun	Mem	Mem	Lamed	Khaf	Kaf	Yod
ס	ן	נ	ם	מ	ל	ך	כ	י
(S)	(N)	(N)	(M)	(M)	(L)	(Kh)	(K/Kh)	(Y)

Tav	Shin	Reish	Qof	Tzadei	Tzadei	Fe	Pei	Ayin
ת	ש	ר	ק	ץ	צ	ף	פ	ע
(T/S)	(Sh/S)	(R)	(Q)	(Tz)	(Tz)	(F)	(P/F)	(Silent)

Psalm 120: This begins the Songs of Ascents (120-134) as part of liturgical activities.

Psalm 121: Another classic while on a pilgrimage or journey to Jerusalem.

Psalm 122: This psalm celebrates Jerusalem, the esteemed Holy City (Zion)

Psalm 123: The covenant community come together and focus (eyes) on the Lord.

Psalm 124: A community psalm of thanks perhaps written by King David showing gratitude to the Lord for deliverance on multiple occasions.

Psalm Book V (Continued)

The last book opens with a series of *Ascent Psalms* attributed to King Solomon and David. Putting it another way, we will observe diverse expressions as Israel sojourns back to Jerusalem. Each of the Psalms presents a unique perspective. I sat in my favorite chair within the bedroom and opened the Bible to Psalm and allowed the Holy Spirit gradually guide me on the eve of presenting this lesson, and what an enlightening journey.

Psalm 125: The mountainous terrain surrounding Jerusalem served as an excellent and majestic way of describing the covenant community's relationship with Yahweh, secured and beautiful. The scepter was a symbol of power that was usually held by the king or queen. Therefore, Israel had no need to fear as long as they spiritually aligned herself with the Most High God. The code of conduct is established and so are the rewards and punishments.

Psalm 126: Israel's chastisement was carried out through the Babylonian Captivity. Therefore, the returnees give a glimpse of what causes laughter versus sorrow. Streams in the south suggest the Negev Desert (the place where the current day African Hebrew Israelite resides). There is a sharp contrast between freedom and bondage.

Psalm 127: This Psalm is a Biblical Classic and attributed to King Solomon. The template for royalty and powerful individuals is displayed when the king dedicated the Temple in Jerusalem. God is the ultimate architect, builder, and security on behalf of Israel. It behooves each of us to be humble and holy versus religious and self-righteous. Family and community should serve as the outlets for blessings. This Psalm reminds me of one of my favorite African Proverbs: "Children are the reward of life." This Psalm and the one following were often quoted by father because he was spiritually grounded and family oriented.

Psalm 128: This Psalm is modeled after Psalm 1 & 2 because they remind us of the blessed man or woman's characteristics. Blessings are spiritual in nature and results in tangible expressions. Olive Plants are plentiful, beneficial, rugged, and perpetual in their environment. Blessings are consummated with peace.

Psalm 129: The Song of Ascents continues. This is the third in succession of family oriented Psalms connected with God's blessings. For example, a typical family will undergo various challenges but in the end the faithful will appreciate these experiences and bless the name of the Lord.

Psalm 130: This Psalm starts off in spiritual tone of Job. It appears God is delaying or removed from assisting His servant during an awkward time. Sin and forgiveness serves as an indication that only God can address this situation. Therefore, the writer encourages Israel to wait patiently on the Lord, her Redeemer.

Psalm 131: We are introduced to an initial Psalm of David in this book that is short but concise. It appears the psalmist is ethical, practical, and spiritual. He goes on to draw a compassionate illustration regarding the soul being calmed in a manner like a baby is weaned from the mother. Therefore, Israel is encouraged to rely on the Lord.

Psalm 132: King David (God's anointed) is referenced as the prime example of a true worshipper simply because he personally worshipped and longed to construct a sanctuary for Yahweh. The writer goes on to give a sense of history, resulting in a place, Jerusalem, Mt. Zion distinguished from all other as the dwelling place.

Psalm 133: Whenever we are asked to behold, it serves as a noteworthy, teachable moment. The Ki-Swahili term *Pamoja* denotes together and *Umoja* means unity. There is no better display in life than to observe spiritual and natural families uniting around common goals and objectives. This reality is compared threefold: precious ointment; priestly role of Aaron, and dew of Mount Hermon. Where are the blessed families on the earth?

Psalm 134: The Psalms gives us a glimpse of true worship and praise at night within the temple. This act of awareness and obedience to God serves as a prime example for all true believers.

Psalm 135: The people are encouraged to praise the Lord because of Israel's relationship via Jacob. The premise for praise also includes God's innate ability to do as He pleases both in heaven and on earth. A brief history illustrating God's intervention on behalf of Israel is shared. Furthermore, idolatry is no match to the Lord God.

Psalm 136: The Psalm shifts from using the term *blessed* with encouragement for the people to give thanks. They should be thankful based upon God's endless goodness and mercies. He is the source of wisdom, light, protection and protection amidst more prominent and established nations that challenged Israel. God has granted land and a heritage to Israel.

Psalm 137: This Psalm is often utilized during African American History Month because there are striking similarities. Enslaved people often find themselves by the rivers that flow through the communities. It appears Israel was captive in Babylon and longed to be in Jerusalem. Meanwhile, the captives delighted in being entertained by each other. Despite the grueling realities of American Chattel Slavery and the realities of the text, God always has a way to speak and re-assures the covenant community their plight is temporary. The Psalm also makes reference to the Edomite's, relatives of Israel assisting the captors during this ordeal. African descendants have always had *Negroes* within the ranks assisting the captors. Nonetheless, there is a day of reckoning or judgment for all acts of unrighteousness.

Psalm 138: There is an appropriate and inappropriate manner to approach the Lord. This Psalm throughout 145 is attributed to King David. Confession and praise are essential ingredients for establishing and maintaining a good relationship with God. The righteous benefit from this relationship, and this posture also enables others to recognize this awesome relationship. Various situations will surface, but God is faithful and delivers, accordingly.

Psalm 139: The Psalm is somewhat long compared to those surrounding it. God examines or evaluate the man and woman who come into His presence. The writer indicates there are no restrictions when it comes to this relationship. For example, there is a tendency to want to withhold certain things. However, in this instance the Psalmist acknowledges God has oversight and dominion both in the visible and invisible world. Therefore, each of us should ask God to purify our heart and soul, in order that you too might stand innocently before the Lord.

Psalms 140: It appears there are accusations and the need to be vindicated. Evil ones are plotting against the righteous in cunning and deceptive tactics. Therefore, the Psalmist petitions God to bring deliverance. Once again. this scenario is similar to Job's experience with his friends.

Psalm 141: This is a Psalm of David depicting a request for Yahweh's immediate attention. He goes on to petition God to show mercy upon his mouth and heart, so they are aligned with spiritual concerns. He acknowledges rebukes and adversities will come, but he welcomes God to direct his path in those moments. The wicked will be punished. and the righteous will be blessed when it is all said and done.

Psalm 142: David wrote this Psalm during a time when he is in the cave (a lowly place fleeing from his enemies). Putting it another way, this is a plaintive prayer. Therefore, God is David's refuge and source.

Psalm 143: David thirsts for God at a time when life seems overwhelming. The Psalm is a prayer of deliverance seeking the righteousness of God. I love the poetry expressed beginning with verse 8, new beginning via the morning, love, good spirit, and His name.

Psalm 144: This is a Royal Psalm of David similar to Psalm 18. The Psalmist wants to know the true and ultimate status of man before God. He realizes the unlimited power of the Lord while man's relationship with God will result in provision and protection both presently and in the future.

Psalm 145: The Psalm is a hymn unto the Lord grounded in His praise and adoration. He goes on to articulate various attributes of the Lord: gracious, everlasting, faithful, righteous and accessible. Therefore, he encourages everyone to praise the Lord.

Psalm 146: The Psalm promotes exhortation unto the Lord versus men and women who claim to have authority and power. The Psalm starts off the *Hallelujah Psalms* throughout the end of the book. References to Jacob and Zion are carefully inserted as a vivid reminder Yahweh is faithful to the covenant community.

Psalm 147: The Psalm takes us down memory lane, includes references to the heavenly elements, and is always mindful of the humble ones. Israel represents the called out one that emerged into a nation, Israel. The Laws of God are established amongst the covenant community; therefore, the Psalmist renders continuous praise.

Psalms 148: Perhaps. this Psalm was used for liturgical purposes, wherein all aspects of creation in heavens and earth are suggested to render praise to the Lord. The writer methodically and skillfully put forth categories of life giving entities both above and beneath to render praise in their unique ways. The ending verse makes reference to and endearing the term *Saints* in relation to God.

Psalm 149: Israel is expected and rightfully so, to praise the Lord. This praise includes new songs, dancing, tambourine and harp. Defeat of Israel's enemies is subsequent to praise and worship.

Psalm 150: The final Psalm is befitting just as we observed a doxology at the ending of each book (41:13; 72:18;-19; 89:52 and 106:48). The Psalmist places great emphasis on praise within the sanctuary and beyond. Praise is supported by His awesome and un-paralleled power. Additional instruments are mentioned as Israel praised the Lord. Everything with breath (Ruah/Nepes) is urged to praise the Lord.

Summary of Psalms

There is no other book in the entire Bible that can make the same claim as Psalms. The book gives us a rhythm or cadence for wholesome living. There are a variety of categories regarding the Psalms, but in essence, we are admonished to learn from life's bitter and sweet moments. Hymns of Praise can only be realized, fully appreciated, and expressed from the community of faith that understands suffering and redemption.

The Psalm is poetry in motion, not static or romanticized. Each of the Psalmists vividly expressed his or her pain or adversity while realizing the faithfulness of God. New Psalms are compiled and expressed, everyday. Therefore, you are the Psalmist who inspires and direct others to praise and worship. Please do not live an unproductive and life. Instead, factor in mishaps, falls, disappointments, and mistakes. However, at the end of the day, let God and others clearly see you as a true worshipper and rendering praise and thanksgiving. Thanks for sharing this journey with me and rest assured the remaining journey will be just as inspiring and informative. If you remain faithful to the critical and literal appreciation of scripture, I can assure you the journey will be rewarding. God bless!

Outline Book of Proverbs

I. Title, Goal and Motto (1:1-7)

II. A Father's Invitation to Wisdom (1:8-9:18)

    A. First paternal appeal: do not join those greedy for unjust gain (1:8-19)

    B. First wisdom appeal (1:20-33)

    C. Second paternal appeal: get wisdom (2:1-22)

    D. Third paternal appeal: fear the Lord (3:1-12)

    E. A hymn to wisdom (3:13-20)

    F. Fourth paternal appeal: walk securely in wisdom (3:21-35)

    G. Fifth paternal appeal: wisdom is a tradition worth maintaining (4:1-9)

    H. Sixth paternal appeal: the two years (4:10-19)

    I. Seventh paternal appeal: maintain a heart of wisdom (4:20-27)

    J. Eight paternal appeals: sexuality (5:1-23)

    K. Warnings relating to securing debts, sloth, and sowing discord (6:1-19)

    L. Ninth paternal appeal: adultery leads to ruin (6:20-35)

M. Tenth paternal appeal: keep away from temptations to adultery (7:1-27)

N. Second wisdom appeal (8:1-36)

O. Lady Wisdom and Lady Folly (9:1-18)

III.   Proverbs of Solomon (10:1-22:16)

IV.   The Thirty Saying of "the Wise" (22:17-24:22)

V.   Further Sayings of "the Wise" (24:23-34)

VI.   Hezekiah's Collection of Solomonic Proverbs (25:1-29:27)

VII. The Sayings of Agur (30:1-33)

VIII. The Sayings of King Lemuel (31:1-9)

IX. An Alphabet of Womanly Excellence: 31:10-31 (also known as Queen Mother Proverb)

Introduction to Proverbs

Proverbs or wisdom statements are entrenched in every culture, generation, and geography throughout the global community. Generally speaking, the Old Testament Hebrew term *Masal* is the same for proverb and may refer to the following meanings: a witty statement; extended parable, vivid illustration, and conveying truth via practical, ethical, and spiritual explanation.

Traditionally, it has been said King Solomon wrote this book. However, it appears he is a major contributor, but there are other contributors who are worthy of recognition. As we take this survey, you will notice both wisdom and foolishness will be depicted in the feminine gender. Nonetheless, you will also note by and large each of the appeals reflects a father and son relationship, whereas the female is in the background playing a lesser role in the instructions.

We will examine this book, but it must be clear from the off-set that the compilation has the spirit of Africa (the Motherland expressed throughout these proverbs.) A few proverbs are listed below.

- Wisdom is wealth. Swahili
- Wisdom is like a baobab tree; no one individual can embrace it. Akan proverb
- The fool speaks, the wise man listens. Ethiopian proverb
- Wisdom does not come overnight. Somali proverb
- The heart of the wise man lies quiet like limpid water. Cameroon proverb

- Wisdom is like fire. People take it from others. Hema (DRC) proverb
- Only a wise person can solve a difficult problem. Akan proverb
- Knowledge without wisdom is like water in the sand. Guinean proverb
- In the moment of crisis, the wise build bridges and the foolish build dams. Nigerian proverb
- If you are filled with pride, then you will have no room for wisdom. African proverb
- A wise person will always find a way. Tanzanian proverb
- Nobody is born wise. African proverb
- A man who uses force is afraid of reasoning. Kenyan proverb
- Wisdom is not like money to be tied up and hidden. Akan proverb

Proverbs reflect collective wisdom and proven paths that are preserved and entrenched in the community as part of the culture. African Proverbs previously stated and Hebraic Proverbs are similar in nature because they cause the listener to pause, listen, and make a choice.

The overall theme of this poetic literature is clearly displayed in the opening chapter because Solomon and the people of God are encouraged and expected to embrace wisdom. This spiritual-reality wisdom is ascertained upon *fearing the Lord.* Once realized, the covenant community will experience a wholesome life vertically (worship) and horizontally (community) speaking.

My curiosity led me to explore what is the numerical relevance or connection associated with the term *Proverbs.*

Interestingly, the terms equates to the number forty-three. If we reduce that number to a single digit, we arrive at the number of completion: seven. Wow! A wise person is a complete individual who reverences (fear the Lord).

Chapter 1: The chapter opens by identifying Israel's most prominent kings: David and his son, Solomon. Verses 1-7 declared wisdom is attainable. However, I like to refer to the spiritual pebbles of instructions, righteousness, justice and equity will lead you to her doorstep. Therefore, it is best to take a posture of humility, listen to, and fear the Lord.

Verse 8 throughout chapter nine has scriptures disclosing a series of wisdom lectures uttered by King David, along with an occasional reference to the mother. Specifically, verses 8-19 admonished the son to be aware of enticements. In other words, this spirit or reality is disguised with things, hasty decision, greed and violence.

The remaining verses (20-33) serve as the first wisdom appeal. This section clearly describes wisdom in the feminine gender. Take note of the judging or judicial side of her wit in verses 24-26. If you ignore her wisdom, then there are consequences. How often have we heard the saying "Listen to your mother's advice?" Wisdom is all over the street but so are the lures and enticements of evil. Listen to her and live. Listen to the other voice and dreadful disasters await you on multiple fronts.

A Father's Invitation to Wisdom

I love the creative and revelatory manner by which these lessons are unfolding. In this session, I will give an overview regarding each chapter throughout chapter nine.

Chapter 2: The chapter emphasizes the value of wisdom, wherein she is likened unto precious minerals, such as silver and gold. In addition, the heart is the safest depository for her. There is a brief reference to adulterous practices, which are foolish along the path of life.

Chapter 3: This chapter is a biblical classic because the emphasis is placed on trust in the Lord. Confidence in the Lord will result in longevity and resounding blessings for generations to come. Meanwhile, the son is advised to pay attention to the abominable and devious person in life.

Chapter 4: The chapter displays wise instruction from a father to his son. Take note of the feminine characteristics of wisdom (verses 3-9). Paying attention to spiritual instructions will propel you through any challenge or reality in life.

Chapter 5: Specific instruction is given regarding adultery. For example, an immoral woman is portrayed displaying a series of enticing gestures in order to grasp the whole picture of this unfaithful spirit. The bottom line is conveyed in verse 15 by being disciplined and drinking from your own cistern. The closing verses 21-23 present the standard for success in life, but the choice must be made by the individual.

Chapter 6: The chapter is properly entitled "Practical Warnings." The writer gives wholesome illustrations of a sluggard versus a responsible man in life. For example, the ant is a great example of showing how to prepare in advance. "

A little sleep, a little slumber, a little folding of the hands to rest, and poverty will come upon you like a robber, and want like an armed man." (6:10-11). Verses 16-19 set forth seven, unethical-behavioral patterns that displease God. The remaining verses give stern warnings against the cunning entrapment of adultery. For example, an illustration is made regarding playing with fire and not getting burned.

Chapter 7: Adultery is the opposite of a faithful and covenant marriage. Therefore, the chapter warns against the adulteress, once again. This marks the 10th paternal appeal to a son surrounded by an environment of temptations. Sin is seductive and persuasive (verse 21), but you will make the appropriate decision if the heart received the Word of God.

Chapter 8: The chapter places emphasis on the blessings of wisdom. Earlier, we observed the adulterous woman enticing and luring the son to act inappropriately; however, wisdom is calling you to embrace her in this instance. She is better than jewel and is embraced by rulers. She is ageless (verse 22-31). Therefore, the son that listens will be positioned in a favorable and blessed place in life.

Chapter 9: This chapter wraps up this section by giving us a contrast between wisdom and folly. Verses 1-12 describe the way of wisdom by referencing the way a firm and impressive house is constructed. Meanwhile, folly is boisterous and welcoming you to enter the chamber and have what the world calls *a good ole time!*

Proverbs Accredited to King Solomon (Chapter 10-22:16)

Chapter 10: The chapter follows the same pattern of the father and mother admonishing the son to live responsibly because God will make provision for the righteous. However, the wicked will not be blessed. Verses 12 & 18 refer to the results of hatred, whereas love has more resounding benefits. Verse 30 reminds us the righteous shall never be removed.

Chapter 11: The writer draws upon a measuring device (scale) in the marketplace in order to illustrate fairness and justice. Deceit and abominable acts may permit you to get what you want at the moment, but it will cause disfavor from the Lord. A great contrast in life is shared in verse 16 between a gracious woman and violent man. Ultimately, the result of the righteous is described as a *Tree of Life.*

Chapter 12: The chapter opens by emphasizing a love for discipline. There is a reference to a model wife and admirable thoughts of the righteous. There is a definite fate and destiny for the wicked although he is right in his own eyes

Chapter 13: A prudent son will take heed to a father's advice, whereas a perverse son will not listen. A lesson on acquiring wealth gradually is better than doing so, hastily. Poverty and disgrace are realities in life, and they are also explained. Verse 22 is a biblical classic that encourages the responsible person to leave an inheritance (property) for the children and grandchildren. Furthermore, the unrighteous assets serve as gate-keepers for the righteous until the Lord deems it necessary to make the transfer.

Chapter 14: This is a model and pivotal chapter because it comes out of the African Tradition, Matriarchal perspective serving at the core of society. A good and firm house is built upon wisdom, not a quick temper or evil intent. Verse 28 is profound: "In the multitude of people is the glory of a king..." Additionally, verse 34 reminds us of what it takes to experience a viable nation or kingdom: righteousness.

Chapter 15: A soft or reasonable tone of voice far outweighs harsh and abrasive language. The tongue, eyes, and heart are used interchangeably as blessed organs throughout life. Therefore, a series of insightful proverbs undergirds this claim.

Chapter 16: The proverbs of Solomon continue with one of my favorite scripture. Plans are inevitable, but we must be patient and prudent in order for the Lord to answer or approve them. Within these plans, we must safeguard against pride (verse18) because a fall is inevitable. Watch your temper because uncontrolled anger will result in unpleasant experiences.

Let me conclude this session with a series of African Proverbs on unity & community:

- Unity is strength, division is weakness. Swahili proverb

- Sticks in a bundle are unbreakable. Bondei proverb
- It takes a village to raise a child. African proverb
- Cross the river in a crowd, and the crocodile won't eat you. African proverb
- Many hands make light work. Haya (Tanzania) proverb
- Where there are many, nothing goes wrong. Swahili proverb
- Two ants do not fail to pull one grasshopper. Tanzanian proverb
- A single bracelet does not jingle. Congolese proverb
- A single stick may smoke, but it will not burn. African proverb
- If you want to go quickly, go alone. If you want to go far, go together. African proverbs

Chapter 17: The chapter gives us a format for a model, righteous home. Poverty is a global reality, but righteousness and integrity will even cause a servant to reign. Whoever makes fun of the poor is insulting the Lord. A template for a true friend is mentioned while the betrayal of a family member causes immeasurable pain. Wisdom prevails and the wicked will have a day in the court of life. The chapter ends by mentioning the value of silence (verse 28).

Chapter 18: There seems to be a tendency to withdraw and rely on your own understanding, but this can be costly. Do not allow your talkative spirit to create trouble (verses 5-8). Throughout life, we are reminded wisdom is true wealth while riches can result in destruction. Verse 21 is a biblical classic because it reminds us the mouth serves as an extension of what is in the heart.

Chapter 19: The Wisdom of Solomon continues and reminds us a poor man can be wise. There is merit in the proverb *Haste makes waste* and referenced in verse 2. Poverty has a tendency to cause family, friends, and neighbors to withdraw from one another or others. We take note of the king's power, unwise son, and a blessed man (verse 14). The person who tends to the poor establishes a relationship with the Lord. Reverence the Lord because this leads to life.

Chapter 20: The chapter opens with a single reference to the nature and result of drinking wine and strong drink. They both have the capacity to sneak upon you, and you are acting out of character before you know it. A reference to the king (see 19:12) and sluggard are mentioned. The chapter presents a series of judgment and benefits of attentive ears and eyes. Verse 27 is profound because it reminds each of us we are an extension of God; therefore, let the lamp shine along our path.

Chapter 21: Planning is as natural as a stream of water for man and woman, but it must be done, righteously. The writer gives a contrast between the lifestyle of the righteous and unrighteous. Verse 19 alludes to a difficult wife in the household being worse than living in the desert. The chapter ends with two, profound proverbs regarding God's infinite wisdom and triumphant spirit.

Chapter 22: The Hebrew term *SEM* denotes name and refers to reputation and identification. Verses 6 and 16 support each other. For example, wise parents will teach his or her child how to reference God and act responsibly in life because there is a tendency to embrace and follow. Verses 17 throughout Chapter 24:22 are similar to the Egyptian Instructions of Amen mope, (also Amenemopet) 1250 BC and are referred as the *Thirty Sayings of the Wise* (verse 20). For example, remember the poor and do not remove the ancient demarcation placed by the fathers.

Speaking of Ancient Egypt, let me to share 9 comparisons regarding the Instructions of Amen mope and the verses in the Book of Proverbs.

Comparison of texts (Wikipedia)

(Proverbs 22:17-18):*"Incline thine ear, and hear the words of the wise, and apply thine heart to my doctrine; for it is pleasant if thou keep them in thy belly, that they may be established together upon thy lips"*

(Amen mope, ch. 1): "Give thine ear, and hear what I say, And apply thine heart to apprehend; It is good for thee to place them in thine heart, let them rest in the casket of thy belly; That they may act as a peg upon thy tongue."

(Proverbs 22:22):*"Rob not the poor, for he is poor, neither oppress (nor* crush*) the lowly in the gate."*

(Amen mope, Ch. 2):"Beware of robbing the poor, and oppressing the afflicted."

(Proverbs 22:24-5): *"Do not befriend the man of anger, nor go with a wrathful man, lest thou learn his ways and take a snare for thy soul."*

(Amen mope, Ch. 10): "Associate neither with a passionate man, nor approach him for conversation; Leap not to cleave to such a one; that terror carry thee not away."

(Proverbs 22:29):*"[if you] you see a man quick in his work, before kings will he stand, before cravens, he will not stand."*

(Amen mope, Ch. 30):"A scribe who is skillful in his business findeth worthy to be a courtier."

(Proverbs 23:1): *"When thou sittest to eat with a ruler, consider diligently what is before thee; and put a knife to thy throat, if thou be a man given to appetite. Be not desirous of his dainties, for they are breads of falsehood."*

(Amen mope, Ch. 23): "Eat not bread in the presence of a ruler, and lunge not forward (?) With thy mouth before a governor (?). When thou art replenished with that to which thou has no right, it is only a delight to thy spittle. Look upon the dish that is before thee, and let that (alone) supply thy need." (See above)

(Proverbs 23:4-5):*"Toil not to become rich, and cease from dishonest gain; for wealth maketh to itself wings, like an eagle that flieth heavenwards"*

(Amen mope, Ch. 7):"Toil not after riches; if stolen goods are brought to thee, they remain not over night with thee. They have made themselves wings like geese. And have flown into the heavens."

(Proverbs 14:7):*"Speak not in the hearing of a fool, for he will despise the wisdom of thy words"*

(Amen mope, Ch. 21):"Empty not thine inmost soul to everyone, nor spoil (thereby) thine influence"

(Proverbs 23:10): *"Remove not the widow's landmark; and enter not into the field of the fatherless."*

(Amen mope, Ch. 6): "Remove not the landmark from the bounds of the field...and violate not the widow's boundary"

(Proverbs 23:12):*"Apply thine heart unto instruction and thine ears to the words of knowledge"*

(Amen mope, Ch. 1):"Give thine ears, hear the words that are said, give thine heart to interpret them."

Chapter 23: The thirty wise saying continues by starting off with the appropriate manner the righteous and humble man should behave in the presence of royalty. Afterward, we are given an array of scenarios in life ranging from listening to the heart, against drunkenness, not being envious, and paying attention to the luring prostitute etc.

Chapter 24: The chapter opens with the 19th sayings of the wise by reminding us to disallow peer pressure dominate your decisions. Wisdom is likened unto a house and serves as the surest way to build upon life. The thirty wise sayings end with verses 21-22 by illustrating a contrast between the responsible and irresponsible person fate and destiny in life. The chapter concludes with additional wise sayings regarding justice and the economy because if you respect both then you will be benefitted by the same.

Let me conclude this lesson with additional African Proverbs for your consideration:

- To be without a friend is to be poor indeed. Tanzanian proverb
- Hold a true friend with both hands. African proverb
- The friends of our friends are our friends. Congolese proverb
- A friend is someone you share the path with. African proverb
- Show me your friend and I will show you your character. African proverb
- Return to old watering holes for more than water; friendship and dreams are there to meet you. African proverb
- Between true friends even water drunk together is sweet enough. African proverb
- A small house will hold a hundred friends. African proverb
- A close friend can become a close enemy. African proverb
- Bad friends will prevent you from having good friends. Gabon proverb

Chapter 25: Solomon's sayings continue throughout the end of chapter 29. The glory of God is discussed by making a comparison with the majesty of a king. Removing dross from silver results in making it more valuable, and the same applies to removing wickedness. A series of illustrations are shared regarding proper etiquette before the king. Gold and jewelry is utilized to depict the supreme value of wisdom. Verse 21 sets the ethical bar high by saying, "If your enemy s hungry, give him bread to eat…" Plus, the final verse gives instruction on self-control.

Chapter 26: Wisdom represents a wholesome and fulfilled life, whereas a fool represents a distorted life. The writer presents a series of analogies regarding the negative outcome of a fool. Verses 4-5 present interesting contrasts regarding the fool; Verses 13-16 give us unique proverbs regarding a sluggard (lazy person). The remaining verses present a series of examples displayed in a person who talks, excessively and carelessly.

Chapter 27: Solomon's wise sayings continue by sharing a few remarks on a boastful person. Notice verses 3-4 utilize two items per verse, but a fool outweighs them, altogether. The remaining verses (11-27) offer a series of proverbial classics. For example, verse 17 is often used in regards to men strengthening each other; verse 18 reminds us faithfulness will be rewarded; and verse 20 reminds us the grave always has room for one more. When all the dust settles, be mindful God will provide for the righteous.

Chapter 28: There is truth in the axiom *save the best for last.* These proverbs appear to be richer and fuller as we come to the close. For example, the stage is set for group behavior and the individual choice. Many of these will stand out, but taking note of verse 5 will help you understand laws of opposites. Listed are a few additional proverbs that stand out: verses 11-12, 18, 22 & 27-28. In other words, these saying supports Fredrick Douglas claim, "Men may not get all they pay for in this world, but they must certainly pay for all for all they get."

Chapter 29: Each of you must remain open-minded for reproof and rebuke when it deems necessary. Wisdom is your best teacher because she is a proven path. Take note of the following verses: 3, 7,11,13,17, 23, & 27 as you make your track through life.

Chapter 30: The chapter opens by introducing a mystical character, Agur. There is no further reference to him throughout the Bible. Of course, there are suggestions offered, including a pen name for King Solomon. Nonetheless, the style differs from the earlier proverbs. For example, the writer asserts despite all the teachings he has not ascertained wisdom. However, there is a profound reverence to the Lord. Verses 7-9 present the only prayer in the book expressed in contrasting views and explanations. Verses 15 throughout the end of the chapter utilize a series of numerical comparison versus being productive and unproductive in life.

Chapter 31: The chapter ends in an impressive style by making reference to both a king and queen. The chapter is uniquely divided into two sections, namely, King Lemuel and The Queen Mother/Virtuous Woman. Verses 1-9 is suggested by some who believe the writer is Queen Bathsheba instructing her son, King Solomon how to behave, namely be watchful of enticing women and strong drink.

Now, the remaining verses have all the trimmings of African influence commonly referred as Queen Mother. It starts off by giving us a prime example of a model wife and mother. She is more valuable than jewels and operates from the posture of wisdom. Her attributes are immeasurable; furthermore, she is admired throughout the community because wisdom is a treasurer.

Let me conclude this book with a series of American African Proverbs:

1. Ain't no use askin' the cow to pour you a glass of milk?

2. All poor people ain't black/ and all black people ain't poor.

3. Death don't see no difference 'tween the big house and the cabin.

4. Dog don't get mad when you say he's a dog.

5. Flies can't fall in a tight-closed pot.

6. Hand plow can't make rows by itself.

7. Heaps of good cotton stocks get chopped up from association with the weeds.

8. I'm not going to lend you a stick to break my head with.

9. If you ask a Negro where he's been, he'll tell you where he's going.

10. If you want to keep something secret from black folks, put it between the covers of a book.

11. A dog that brings a bone will carry one.

12. Money talks-everything else walks.

13. You can read my letter but you can't read my mind.

14. Empty wagon makes the loudest noise.

15. One monkey don't stop no show.

16. God does not bless mess.

17. Old Satan couldn't get along without plenty of help.

18. Old used-to-do-it-this-way don't help none today.

19. Romance/ without finance/ don't stand a chance.

20. Talkin' 'bout fire doesn't boil the pot.

21. Tell me whom you love, and I'll tell you who you are.

22. The blacker the berry the sweeter the juice.

23. We ain't what we want to be; we ain't what we gonna be; but thank God, we ain't what we was

24. A man who does not respect his own mother is absolutely no good.

25. The worm does not see anything pretty in the robin's song.

Outline of Ecclesiastes

I. Introduction and Theme (1:1-3)

II. First Catalog of "Vanities" (1:4-2:26)

    A. The "vanity" of the natural world (1:4-11)

    B. The "vanity" of wisdom and knowledge (1:12-18)

    C. The "vanity" of pleasures, possessions, and accomplishments (2:1-11)

    D. More on the "vanity" of wisdom (2:12-17)

    E. The "vanity" of labor (2:18-26)

III. Poem: A Time for Everything (3:1-8)

IV. Fear God, the Sovereign One (3:9-15)

V. Second Catalog of "vanities" (3:16-4:16)

    A. The "vanity of mortal life" (3:16-4:3)

    B. More on the "vanity of labor" (4:4-12)

    C. More on the "vanity of wisdom" (4:13-16)

VI. Fear God, the Holy and Righteous One (5:1-7)

VII. Life "Under the Sun" (5:8-7:24)

    A. Injustice (5:8-9)

    B. Greed vs. contentment (5:10-6:9)

    C. Wisdom for living "under the sun" (6:10-7:24)

VIII. The Heart of the Problem: Sin (7:25-29)

IX. More on Life "under the Sun" (8:1-12:7)

A. Wisdom in dealing with foolish authorities (8:1-9)
B. The importance of fearing God (8:10-13)
C. The limits of human knowledge (8:14-17)
D. The unpredictability of life and certainty of death (9:1-6)
E. Finding enjoyment as circumstances allow (9:7-10)
F. More on the unpredictability of life (9:11-12)
G. The paths of wisdom and foolishness (9:13-11:6)
    1. The power of wisdom (9:13-18)
    2. Proverbs concerning wisdom and foolishness (10:1-20)
    3. Wise practices in light of the unpredictability of life (11:1-6)

H. Aging and the "vanity" of mortal life (11:7-12:7)

X. Final Conclusion and Epilogue (12:8-14)

Introduction to Ecclesiastes

Asking questions are appropriate as we take the journey through this poetic/wisdom literature. Where do we begin, and what can we say about this unique compilation? Ecclesiastes is one of the 24 official books of the Tanakh (Hebrew Bible). It is also placed in the Wisdom Literature, also known as the Ketuvim (The Writings) in the Canonized Bible. The current title *Ecclesiastes* is the Latin translation of the Hebrew term *Qoheleth* denoting teacher or gatherer who lectures before a select assembly, known as *Qahal*. The author is anonymous, but King Solomon is traditionally held to be the author, especially since the opening verse alludes to a son of King David.

Please be mindful the phrase "Son of David" is used in Matthew 1:20 for referring to Joseph. In other words, the phrase is commonly linked to anointed men within the Davidic Dynasty and lineage. Personally, I support the notion of an anonymous writer who skillfully piques the interest of the reader to assume this is the product of King Solomon. The book is full of proverbs but crafted in thought-provoking and unconventional perspectives on life.

The terms *Preacher* and *Vanity* are used throughout the text as a reminder that an authorized spiritual agent is lecturing before an audience that is expected to embrace wisdom. We will discover the term *vanity*. Scripturally, the word is found throughout the Old Testament, but it is more prevalent in this book. It basically means a vapor, nothingness, emptiness, trouble or wickedness, etc. Prior to exploring the chapters let us observe the numerical or *Gem atria* method of measuring a word. For example, the term *Ecclesiastes* contains twelve letters (government or divine administration). Even further, we would arrive at thirty-eight if we were to add the letter. We can reduce this number to a single digit by adding three plus eight and arriving at eleven (disorder), and one plus one equals two (union and division). Therefore, life is like a vapor: transient, wherein you can be blessed or cursed; embrace wisdom or folly.

Remember, the book is placed in a philosophical (ability to think or insight) or theosophical (God's Wisdom) format. In other words, pertinent questions and soul-searching statements will be presented while opting not to give an immediate explanation or answer. However, it is my hope you will be more prudent, patient, inquisitive, and spiritual by the time we finish this journey.

Chapter 1: This chapter opens by establishing a link to Israel's greatest king, David. Therefore, this claim alone alludes to an official document that is noteworthy of paying attention. The chapter also begins a catalog or series of ways we should observe vanity in this world. The claim "All is vanity" grasps your attention and will prompt a great discussion. Verses 4-11 speak to the natural or universal way things happens and reminds us (vs. 10) it has been done before. The remaining verses share a few comments on the Vanity of Wisdom. Perhaps, he is suggesting it requires humility and awareness to embrace wisdom, but this does not change the folly and pain one has yet to encounter.

Chapter 2: The explanation on vanity continues. The chapter opens by presenting the vanity of self-indulgence wherein the Preacher went about acquiring whatever was on his heart, i.e. wine folly, vineyards, slaves, singers and concubines, etc. Both the heart and eyes may prompt you to acquire things because at the time you have the resources to do so. However, there is truth in knowing each of these acquisitions may bring immediate gratification, boost your ego and illuminate your status in life, but in the end, things cannot bring happiness.

Chapter 3: From childhood I have observed this chapter utilized time and time again during a funeral. Actually, the chapter has several sub-titles, such as:

- A time for Everything – Verses 1-8
- The God-Given Task – Verses 9-15
- From Dust to Dust – Verses 16-22

In essence, there is an occasion for everything, including good and evil. The biblical orientation of time has to do with a precise, definite, and identifiable period. Verses 2-8 present fourteen (deliverance), contrasting realities disbursed in life that give a comprehensive picture of reality. I would like for you to observe the following: They begin with a positive reality (born) and end with a positive reality (peace). Therefore, there will be multiple and diverse challenges to deal with between birth and the time or state of peace.

The next section speaks from the experience that everything is ultimately beautiful in its time (verse 11) once you are aware. Furthermore, it is stated God's plan cannot be altered.

The latter section gives an interesting, theological perspective in the Old Testament. The Preacher is stating there is an irony or paradoxical way of looking at wickedness and justice because they are occupied by the wrong person, occasionally. He ends by giving a perspective of man and beast's deaths and final states. Both comes from the dust and breathe in a similar manner wherein both will die.

Chapter 4: This chapter presents a discourse on the reality of evil under the sun. We also observe a series of proverbs in a familiar format. Oppression and laziness are realities in life. Unity and cooperation in life have benefits in life. Lastly, the poor and wise youth appeared before the king, just as all of us will have to give an account of our stewardship on earth.

Chapter 5: The chapter opens by reminding the assembly to fear and reverence God by giving a scenario on how to approach or worship God. For example, the concept of a vow stems from the Old Testament spiritual mandate of the Votive Offering. Generally speaking, a vow is a pledge or dedication for a fixed period. Therefore, be mindful what you promise before God and the community of faith. The remaining verses speak about wealth and honor. Money is a means of exchange based upon a desire or need for goods. However, money alone will not satisfy. It is far better to act and negotiate in such a manner, whereby you can rest peacefully. Wealth may create privileges and permit you to acquire what you want ought to be viewed as a gift from God.

Chapter 6: This serves as the shortest chapter in the book but contains a profound lesson. He gives several scenarios of vanity. For example, a man was given status but unable to enjoy the benefits that came alone with it; a man lives a ripe age but dies unhappy and no burial; we have strange appetites that often results in not being satisfied and lastly there is nothing new so what is really good for man?

Chapter 7: All the proverbial books return to the prevailing contrast in life, namely wisdom versus folly (Eccl. 2:12; Ps. 45:8). Fate and circumstances may be unwanted but maintaining a godly character and integrity outweigh pleasures. Take note of the term, *better* being used as a reminder of that which is appropriate versus inappropriate. Verse 13 gives an interesting point that presents an ongoing discussion regarding the ability of a person to change. He goes on to mention an unrighteous man lives a long time while the righteous dies prematurely, and that too is puzzling or vanity. Verses 25f draws upon the prevailing contrast of a man being influenced by a cunning woman.

Chapter 8: Once again, wisdom is esteemed, and the man who adheres to her teaching is distinguished. In addition, the writer reminds the assembly the king is a representative of God on behalf of the people. Therefore, be cautious in appearing before him and always show respect. Life will present multiple faces but no man can manipulate the spirit and evade death (verse 8). Verses 10-13 reminds us the man who reverence God will ultimately do well in life, however, it may appear the wicked is getting by. The remaining verses remind us of Job's friends and their discourses claiming to know God. In other words the Preacher eludes that at the end of the day we will be baffled at the things that happen in life.

Chapter 9: The chapter reminds us death is inevitable, righteous, and unrighteous. The writer's perspective does not embrace resurrection theology (verse 5). Therefore, he encourages the assembly to enjoy life to the fullest because even "a living dog is better than a dead lion." Enjoy life with all the amenities, and (most certainly) enjoy your wife. Verse 10 is a Biblical Classic: "Whatever your hand finds to do, do it with all your might." Do not procrastinate and waste precious time during your lot or portion in life. The chapter ends by repeating wisdom is greater than folly. Yes, a poor, wise man's advice enabled the city he dwelled in to be saved.

Chapter 10: The chapter presents no less than seventeen proverbs covering a wide range of subjects with profound lessons in each. Remarks on several are listed. Verse 8 suggests evil intent is like a boomerang. Verse 19 says each of these is presented favorably such as bread satisfies hunger, wine makes you cheerful, and money carries influence regarding exchange.

Chapter 11: Life may seem to be unpredictable but the wise man will overcome and make good even in adverse situations. Manage what you have and do not let the weather patterns, cloud or winds cause you to procrastinate.

Plant the seeds in life and give your best daily but always factor in challenges because youth and aging are re-occurring patterns.

Chapter 12: The Preacher concludes this book in an impressive fashion. Remember or consider embracing a spiritual life that includes wisdom because evil is inevitable. Evil is trouble or interruption that is unwelcomed. The analogy of the youth and aged man serves as a powerful illustration of things gradually changing. For example, there comes a time when the eyes and ears will not allow you to be sensitive to the things around you. Sometimes we call this transitioning, *Father Time.* Reverence God and follow the spiritual mandates being taught through nature and teachers. Verse 13 is simply profound, "The end of all matter, all has been heard. Fear God and keep his commandments for this are the whole duty of man....."

Summary: Learn to talk less and observe more. Philosophy and theology combined is called theosophy. Therefore, I suggest you ask pertinent questions throughout life because this illustrates you are paying attention. Embrace theology by allowing your faith to seek clarity while it guides you. Wisdom will join you and undergird you when decisions need to be made, but this will only occur if you remain patient, humble, and obedient. Vanity or vapor (as he calls it) is nothing more than a perspective. What you do with your life has a lot to do with what you really know about life. I opt for wisdom versus folly and at the end of the day firmly believe I will look back and appreciate the journey. God bless!

Outline Song of Solomon

I. Title: The Best of Songs (1:1)

II. The Lovers Yearn for Each Other (1:2-2:17)

III. The Shepherdess Dreams (3:1-6:3)

IV. The Lovers Yearn for Each Other Again (6:4-8:4)

V. The Lovers Join in Marriage (8:5-14)

Introduction to Song of Solomon

This poetic/wisdom literature is romantic, sensuous and conveys a profound love affair that accentuates beauty via a courtship and marriage. Traditionally, scholars believed King Solomon compiled this during his reign in the 10th Century B.C., and this is supported in referencing his name within verse one. Perhaps, this is true and perhaps not; however, his name is placed in verse 1. Nonetheless, the text associated with his legacy and kingship will be readily accepted.

It is well documented King Solomon had multiple wives, including the Pharaoh's daughter along with a line of harems. Therefore, the wisdom expressed throughout this book reflects someone with vast experience and having multiple, intimate relationships. Even further, it is suggested the book deals with a period during his diplomatic and spiritual journey as King of Israel. Please take note of the shepherd (1:7) and shepherdess (1:8) identified. Perhaps, a deeper message refers to Yahweh's un-wavering love for Israel. The book further serves as a clear and vivid reminder we are discovering an African voice, including Solomon and the women he interfaces. Blacks have been blessed with poetry, creativity, and a profound sense of spirituality.

Chapter 1: The chapter discloses back and forth romantic expressions of an attraction and love affair between two, identified as *she* and *he*. However, there is a third party, *others* that is suggested to be a chorus echoing or reaffirming the expressions. Verses 2-7 (with the exception for the latter, 1:4b) have the passionate yearning of the female longing to be with the male. Verse 5 is a Biblical Classic highlighting the beauty and sacredness in blackness. Historically, Kedar was a son of Ishmael (Gen. 25:13; Isa. 21:16, 42 and 49:28-29). The Tents of Kedar refers to the black goats among the semi-nomadic tribes. Verses 8-9 give a response by guiding her to him. He goes on to indicate his attraction is compared to the distinguished/selected mares associated with Pharaoh's chariot. The discourse continued throughout the chapter and makes reference to perfume, plants, trees, doves, and pure love.

Chapter 2: The chapter opens by referencing two admirable flowering plants: rose and lily. Sharon was noted for a bountiful display of these flowers. She goes on to draw upon a delicious apple from the forest along with raisins during a banquet. Her beloved is compared to a gazelle gracefully moving through the terrain. Verses 11-13 describe springtime and the various activities associated with her, such as flowers, turtledove, figs and vineyard. Even further the character displayed in the dove and fox is compared to her beloved. However, there is an irony in the fox that can be evasive and a pest in the field. The chapter ends esteeming him like a gazelle in the cleft of the rock and a desire for her beloved to turn inward and embrace her as a soulmate.

Chapter 3: The colorful and romantic discourse from the shepherdess continues. Verses 1-4 indicate she is dreaming and longing to be with her lover. Therefore, she gets up late at night and moves about the city looking for him. Once he is found, she brings him back to her place. The description changed in verses 5-11 as if we are witnessing an engagement and wedding procession. Royal ornaments and a glorious setting are displayed. Lebanon is referenced because this is one of the sacred & utopian places that remind us of the Garden of Eden (sanctuary).

Chapter 4: The poetry is simply amazing, wherein the shepherd is describing the beauty of his beloved in specific details. Reference to locks is a clear indication of someone Black and the notion of being fair reflects the various shades of blackness i.e. ebony, mahogany, indigo, and blue-black etc. One commentary describes this as if we are intruding upon a private and intimate affair. Verses 8-14 describe the natural environment, including leopards & bear (no longer in that area). He goes on to mention organic vegetation and notices the pomegranate is healthy for the heart as well as a symbol of nobility and priesthood.

Let me expound briefly on the pomegranate. The fruit is a symbol of marriage and everlasting life. The health benefits are too numerous to mention, but a few features are being anti-inflammatory and preventive of heart disease. It was a symbol of the Moors and the priesthood during Moses and Aaron's era required the priest ephod to display pomegranate (Ex. 28:31-35 & 1 Kings 7:20-21) on the garments. A great book to read on the natural and spiritual implications of this fruit and more is entitled *Eden: The Biblical Garden Discovered in East Africa* by Gert Muller.

Other spices and wholesome foods are mentioned in comparison to the beloved. The remaining verses describe the bride as a garden accompanied with streams and refreshing wind. All of this serves as a reminder of a love affair between Adam and Eve in the Garden of Eden.

Chapter 5: Theologically speaking, the garden should be viewed as a sanctuary or nourishing haven. We note in every description there are nourishing plants and herbs such as myrrh. Interestingly, verses 2-7 indicate there seems to be a shift in the closeness and warm embrace. All marriages will undergo challenges and alienation (verses 6-7). However, there is an appeal to be restored. Verses 10-11 give us a profound illustration of blackness in the purest manner. Throughout the challenges in marriage, the couple should emerge as friends and not just lovers.

Chapter 6: The marriage is consummated, and the challenges have emerged; nevertheless, the love remains in place. The beloved has gone to the garden and take in the spices and lilies. Tirzah (a city northeast of Jerusalem) was noted as a resort, beauty, and pleasure. We note the reference to many wives (polygamy) in verse 8 while illustrating an unswerving love for the shepherdess (verse 13).

Chapter 7: The romance continues with a pleasant description of the body from top to bottom. Remember the Bible is not written for history and geography, but both are frequently mentioned. For example, the text casually mentions a place called *Bath-rabbim.* A few commentaries are listed: "The Shulamite maiden's eyes are likened to "the pools in Heshbon, by the gate of Bath-rabbim." (SS 7:4) Heshbon was a city in the territory of Gad, but it was assigned to the Levites. (Jos 21:38, 39) Some believe the name Bath-rabbim is the name of a gate of Heshbon facing toward the city of Rabbah (modern 'Amman) to the NE while others suggest that Bath-rabbim (meaning "Daughter of the Many") is used figuratively to mean the populous city of Heshbon itself, and that the gate is so called because many people passed in and out of the city or gathered at the gate for assembly. Around the present ruins of the city, evidence remains of ancient pools as well as of a large reservoir. The poetic description gives an apt picture of limpid, serene beauty seen in the shining eyes of the Shulamite, the city gate perhaps representing the forehead.

It appears this prolonged marriage helps create new and innovative expressions of love in various locations such as the field, village, and vineyard. Once again, the garden and organic plants are frequently mentioned.

Chapter 8: From antiquity and currently in many places throughout the world public affection or romance is frowned upon. However, in this chapter the lover desired to openly express her love for her lover just as a child is openly breastfed. This chapter concludes with powerful illustrations of love, such as verses 6-7. Love is strong and can cause jealousy. Love is like a fire and a seal and love is more valuable than the house and contents therein.

There is a section where the Shulamite reflects as a young girl with her brothers trying to safeguard her along the right path (verses 8-10). An interesting scenario is disclosed, wherein Solomon (the king) is privileged to have access to much, yet there is respect for those who have less (verses 11-12). The chapter ends by describing the marriage became stronger and more creative instead of becoming dull and unattractive.

Summary: Both the Old and New Testaments give us interesting examples of a relationship between man and woman. In addition, the Bible illustrates the manner, whereby Yahweh marries Israel and Christ marries the Church.

The writer(s) of Song of Solomon discloses an eyeopener when it comes to engagement, courtship, and marriage. Upon marrying, the flame of love should not run out but rather remain open to creative and passionate means of expression. The book is accredited to King Solomon and a Shulamite Maiden. Throughout the book, we observed the motivational principle of God: love always finds a new way to express itself.

Several themes are listed you might consider under the watchful eyes of God throughout a relationship: Sex; Love; Commitment; Beauty, and Problems.   Exploring these themes within your covenant relationship will enable you to become grounded and faithful.

Lastly, I truly appreciate this book because it presents a profound spiritual message via a romantic relationship steeped in the African experience. I also find it to be ironic when it comes to American Africans being presented as if we have abandoned our families and do not know how to be romantic. The text has been preserved in a revealing fashion and it is up to you to go deeper and research the data because there is much more than what meets the eyes in this book.

Conclusion: This concludes the Wisdom/Poetic (Ketuvim) section of the Bible. As you can see wisdom is a proven and eternal path. However, the wise will always factor in foolishness and stupidity as he or she travels.

There is so much we do not know and much of this is due largely in part to diabolical ideologies and schools of thoughts embedded in religious teachings. Truth is eternal and will always be there to discover. However, the truth can only be discovered if there is a spirit of humility and the opening for awareness.

The truth is human life and civilization began in Africa, followed by Asia, Australia, Europe, and lastly the Americas. This is painful for some, but it is refreshing for others. I take delight in presenting this commentary because the readers will have a refreshing approach to ancient materials. It is never appropriate to become stagnated or myopic in your perspective. The Spirit of Truth is eternal and creative in nature. I remain open and attentive to the path that leads to eternal life, within these earthen vessels.

The volume that follows this section in the Bible is commonly called the books of prophecy. I can assure you that presentation will follow the same format, refreshing, and soul-stirring revelations. The Bible remains relevant in contemporary times because she is not restricted to the era in which she was compiled. Simply stated, she addressed the past, gives insights about contemporary realities, and gives directives to the future. Putting it another way, the Bible is a spiritual roadmap that involves historical and temporal settings in order to create eternal truths here on earth. Now, the journey continues. God bless!

Bible Survey Examination: Wisdom Literature

1. Describe the overall theme of the book of Wisdom Literature.

2. Can you list the five books in this section?

3. Where does the story of Job take place and who were these people?

4. What is the overall theme of Job?

5. Describe the types of attacks that came upon Job?

6. What lessons have you learned about suffering as a result of studying Job?

7. What caused the shift in Job's three friend's intent and their comments?

8. Describe the overall intent and behavior of Job's friends.

9. List your thoughts on Satan and God's conversations regarding Job.

10. List your comments on Job chapter 19.

11. Explain forgiveness upon the basis of Job's last chapter.

12. What does the term *psalm* means?

13. Explain why *Psalms* is the most widely read book in the Bible?

14. How many books/sections are in *Psalms*?

15. The Psalm is modeled after the _____.

16. Give the breakdown of the books/sections in the Psalm?

17. Describe a Lament Psalm.

18. List and define 3 additional Psalms.

19. Name three Psalmists besides David.

20. Give a critical and literal interpretation of Psalm 23.

21. List and define 5 types of Psalms.

22. Explain who Korah and Asaph were?

23. Why do you suppose David is the most heralded psalmist?

24. What is a proverb?

25. Most of the Proverbs in the Bible are attributed to

_____.

26. Name two terms that contrasts with wisdom?

27. The thirty proverbs in chapter 22 are similar to which ancient people?

28. Give me your thoughts on Proverbs 19th chapter.

29. Explain Proverb 31 and the Queen Mother reference.

30. The term *Qahal* in Ecclesiastes is defined as

_____.

31. The term *Qoheleth* in Ecclesiastes is defined as

_____.

32. How would you describe the overall intent of this book?

33. What is meant by vapor or vanity?

34. Explain the text: Eccl. 3:1-8

35. Share your thoughts regarding theology and philosophy.

36. Song of Solomon is describing a relationship between

_____.

37. What is the overall theme of this book?

38. Give me several illustrations supporting blackness in the book.

39. Describe the comparison between Solomon's love and Yahweh's love for Israel.

40. What is the overall intent of Wisdom/Poetic Literature in the Bible?

41. Based upon these lessons can you discuss who the Hebrew Israelites are?

42. Can you briefly describe the difference between Jews and Hebrew Israelites?

43. Describe the role of songs and poetic expressions in the community of the oppressed.

44. Which character impressed you the most: Job, David, or Solomon? Please explain?

45. Explain faith and works within the grace of God.

46. Share your favorite Psalm and why?

47. How would you describe these lessons?

48. Do you have a better understanding of the critical and literal approaches to biblical studies?

49. How do you explain the relevance of the Bible in contemporary times?

50. Can you discuss why there has been a longstanding attempt to suppress commentaries similar to this one?

www.ingramcontent.com/pod-product-compliance
Lightning Source LLC
Chambersburg PA
CBHW072024040426
42447CB00009B/1714